Joan Nestle is an author, editor, ar
Co-founder of the Lesbian Herstory
and largest collection of its kind ir
plores in her work the crossroads where sex, memory
and history meet. Her award winning publications
include *A Restricted Country* (Firebrand Books), *The
Persistent Desire; A Femme-Butch Reader* (Alyson
Publications), *Women on Women 1, 2 and 3* (Plume
Books) and most recently *Sister and Brother: Lesbians
and Gay Men Talk about their Lives Together*
(HarperSanFrancisco). For the last thirty years she has
been a teacher of writing in the SEEK Program at
Queens College, CUNY. She was the first recipient of the
David A. Kessler Award for Life Long Achievement in
the Gay and Lesbian Community, presented by CLAGS,
the Center for Lesbian and Gay Studies at the Graduate
Center of CUNY, and in 1994 she received the Sappho
Award for Literary Distinction from Astraea, a national
Lesbian funding group. She is presently working on a
collection of international Lesbian short fiction and a
new collection of her own writings, *A Fragile Union.*

A RESTRICTED COUNTRY
Documents of Desire and Resistance

Joan Nestle

 An Imprint of HarperCollins*Publishers*

In memory of Carol Betty Lipman,
Sonny Wainwright, and Regina Nestle

Dedicated to Deborah Edel,
who taught me the passion of decency

Pandora
An Imprint of HarperCollins*Publishers*
77–85 Fulham Palace Road,
Hammersmith, London W6 8JB

First published by Firebrand Books, New York 1987
Published by Sheba Feminist Publishers, London 1988
This edition published by Pandora 1996

Selections from this book have appeared previously
in the following periodicals: *Bad Attitude, Bad Apple
Dyke (B.A.D.) News, Body Politic, Common Lives
Lesbian Lives, Conditions, Gay Community News,
Heresies, Lesbian Connection, On Our Backs,
13th Moon*, and *Sinister Wisdom*

Joan Nestle asserts the moral right to
be identified as the author of this work

A catalogue record for this book
is available from the British Library

ISBN 0 04 440945 1

Printed in Great Britain
by Caledonian International Book Manufacturer, Glasgow

Contents

Acknowledgments

The following Lesbian, gay and feminist publications gave my work a public life: *Bad Attitude, B.A.D News, Body Politic, Common Lives/ Lesbian Lives, Conditions, Gay Community News, Heresies, Lesbian Connection, On Our Backs, 13th Moon, Sinister Wisdom.*

I thank Nancy K. Bereano for her interest in my work and her courage in wanting the whole manuscript, the erotic and the theoretical.

I acknowledge and cherish the support of my friends who have stayed with me through illness and through self-doubt, who have stood beside me when others have turned away, who through the dignity of their person and the power of their work taught me what was possible; Deborah Edel, Judith Schwarz, Ava Alterman, Eileen Margaret, Susan McConnaughy, Naomi Holoch, Naomi Replansky, Marcyne Maurice, Linda Levine, Phyllis Rosechild, Kathleen Yemm, Leslie Kahn, Rota Silverstrini, Jan Boney, Pam Parker, Paula Grant, Marsha Labovitz, Mabel Hampton, Liz Kennedy, Jonathan Katz, Morgan Gwenwald, Paula Webster, June Bobb, Chub Fontinell, Maxene Kupperman-Guiñals, Francisco Guiñals, Jewelle Gomez, Cheryl Clarke, Adrienne Rich, Madeline Davis, Jo Deal, Carol Karlman, Pat Califia, Ann Snitow, Paige Gillies, Dorothy Allison, John D'Emilio, Alan Berube, Irare Sabasu, Claire Moed, the Amazon Autumn women, the Lesbian Illness Support Group, my poetry group, the Lesbian Herstory Archives work group, and my students.

Preface

History, like so many other things, has been re-defined in the past two decades. More and more we are learning to listen to the individual and collective voices of the people who were once seen only as the victims of history, or as the backdrop for the drama of the rich, the powerful, the heads and tails of state. Like painted trees in robust operas, the baker and the housewife, the whore and the clerk just stood there while Kings and Queens sang their dreams and dirges around them. Now we have grassroots history projects documenting a vast range of human life, and I have been lucky enough to be a participant in one of these projects – the grassroots Lesbian and gay history movement. In doing this work, I have learned such things as the complexity and diversity of resistance, the nonchalance of courage, and the tenacity of those who are different. And one thing more: that for gay people, history is a place where the body carries its own story.

I would like this book to be read as history, these stories and essays to be documents of a flesh and a spirit that lived through and were changed by their times: the McCarthy fifties, the activist sixties, the institution-building of the seventies, and the renewed social struggle of the eighties. These times leave their mark both on the body and the imagination, but it is the body that has been most often cheated out of its own historical language, the body that so often appears as the ahistorical force that we simply carry with us until, for those of us born healthy, it tumbles us to the earth of restricted movement.

But my body made my history – all my histories. Strong and tough, it allowed me to start work at thirteen; wanting, it pushed me to find the lovers that I needed; vigorous and resilient, it carried me the fifty-four miles from Selma to Montgomery. Once desire had a fifties face; now it is more lined. But still when I walk the streets to protest our military bullying of Central America, or the Meese Commission on Pornography, or apartheid in South Africa and here, my breasts and hips shout their own slogans. As a woman, as a Lesbian, as a Jew, I know that much of what I call history others will not. But answering that challenge of exclusion is the work of a lifetime.

The women's movement understood the need for a profound breaking of boundaries when it embraced the slogan 'the personal is political'. I would like to carry it one step further: if the personal is political, the more personal is historical. The more personal demands attention be paid to how we fill our days and nights as we participate in any given economic system, how our flesh survives under different political systems, how we humanize gender tyranny, how we experience womanness and maleness in all the superstructures of class and race.

Erotic writing is as much a documentary as any biographical display. Fantasies, the markings of the erotic imagination, fill in the earth beneath the movement of great social forces; they tell deep tales of endurance and reclamation. They are a people's most private historic territory. This is why I always wince when a gay activist says we are more than our sexuality, or when Lesbian culture celebrants downplay lust and desire, seduction and fulfilment. If we are the people who call down history from its heights in marble assembly halls, if we put desire into history, if we document how a collective erotic imagination questions and modifies monolithic societal structures like gender, if we change the notion of woman as self-chosen victim by our public stances and private styles, then surely no apologies are due. Being a sexual people is our gift to the world.

I, and many others like me, were never the leaders of major events or the presidents of national organizations. We filled the

ranks, walked the streets, answered the phones, did the mail-
ings, but it was the collective history of our bodies' desire that
helped forge the changes to come. When I joined in founding
the Lesbian Herstory Archives, it was not because I wanted
power or money or fame, but because all the experiences of my
different identities led me there: my Jewish self that knew
memory was a holy thing, never to be bartered or sold; my old
femme self that knew the sacredness of a scorned courage; my
new feminist self that wanted the delight of a women-only
creation; my socialist self that believed all resources must be
shared; my teacher self that had been taught by First World
students the burden of colonization and the pain of exile; my
psychological self that called on me to carry my mother and her
loneliness into my own conflicts about security and freedom.
And, like a hemp rope binding the parts together, ran my sexual
self, taking on all these forms of being and rearranging them in
stunning new ways. Out of this came the Lesbian Herstory
Archives and this book.

On July 1, 1986 the Reagan Supreme Court, also invoking
history, empowered the states to put Lesbians and gay men in jail
for making love in the privacy of their homes. I mourn this use of
history, this resurrection of ancient bigotry, to give life to
contemporary fear and hatred of us. History, that huge conglom-
eration of people and events, is a tricky thing to invoke. Often
one people's history to be glorified and celebrated is another
people's hell. One cannot have unquestioning faith in history; it
is, as the Italian philosopher said, a paradoxical force rather than
a progressive one. We choose the history that we say is ours and
by so doing, we write the character of our people in time.

On June 29, 1986 we marched in New York to proclaim
our gay pride. One of the chants we chose to throw into the
summer air was, 'From Stonewall to Soweto, the people are
resisting.' Let this be the history we make ours.

Joan Nestle
December 1986
New York City

Introduction To New Edition

When I read this book today, fifteen years after its first piece was written, I wonder at how naked I was willing to be. Silences haunted me then – the invisibility of my working class butch-femme community, the muting of the sexual and the dissociation of desire from history. I wanted to tell another story, one of historical and personal reclamation. I did not know if my journey would have meaning to others. I did know that some pieces would be unsettling to the prevailing lesbian feminist positions of the mid-seventies, but I wanted to keep complexities alive in a time of rhetorical sternness. This more complicated portrait of a Lesbian's life, I believed, could only strengthen the insights of feminism.

A Restricted Country was never conceived of as a book. In the mid-seventies, after I became ill, a group of friends formed a writing group that met at my apartment to keep me going. The first story I wrote, 'Mara's Room' came from a place of resistance in me that I did not even know I could make use of – the hot hushed moments of entry and coming. Every time my illness dragged me down, I fought back with a story about a transgressive body. These writings, and those growing out of my work with the Lesbian Herstory Archives, found homes in the lesbian feminist and gay journals and newspapers of the seventies and eighties.

Little by little, I learned from my own memory how a life takes shape. Images from my early queer years of the fifties flooded me. My words were born on the bathroom line of the Sea Colony, a working class butch-femme bar of the 1950s and 60s. This searing ritual of humiliation and pride was the primary contradiction behind my historical vision. Today when I read that piece to younger and younger audiences, I tell them, 'May you never endure it, may I never forget it.'

In 1982, I wrote the essay, 'Butch-Fem Relationships: Sexual Courage in the 1950s' for *Heresies*, a feminist art journal, plunging me into the centre of the sex wars. After ten years of lesbian feminist organizing, I needed to come home, but what was home to me was an anathema to others. In 1986, Nancy Bereano of Firebrand Books suggested that I put my writings together into a manuscript and send it to her. Together we gave form and shape to *A Restricted Country*. I will always be deeply grateful to the small presses and publishers who risked so much to put my words in print.

Over the years, *A Restricted Country* has brought me many readers: readers who took Regina as their own, readers who spread their legs with me, readers who found a moment of freedom in a new terrain. To other readers, however, the book presented a threatening geography. One leading lesbian feminist thinker held me responsible for ushering in a new time of decadence. Copies mysteriously disappeared before they could make their way to library shelves and painfully, some women's bookstores would not stock it. In the back of a recent encyclopaedia on gay and Lesbian writers, I appear in the small column of pornographers.

And even I, now, sometimes fail my own words. In April of this year, I was reading in a straight bookstore in Chelsea in New York. A member of the audience asked me to read the piece about anal love making. With customers milling about, I started to pour the words into the air, the image of a woman's ass opening for her lover's fingers. Leaning against the wall, my body tired with a long day, I tried not to think about the roving strangers and the puckered flesh, but half way into the story, I had to stop. These words, born in passionate places, are even more precious to me now in my fifty-fifth year than when I first wrote them. They are dreams of the body made from real moments. They are intimacies made public because the fragility of touch and the weight of history haunt me.

Much has changed in the years between the first edition of this book and now. Butch and femme have become highly orchestrated motifs of queer theory. Gender bends and sways, cross dressing is celebrated – Lesbian erotic writing abounds, at least in the United States. The communities in whose name I wrote have found other loving voices to preserve them. But the tensions between what governments will allow and what the flesh might seek, between how a woman is constructed and what a Lesbian is, between histories marked by class and race, between the world-wide struggle for autonomy of difference and the forces of ethnic cleansing shatter hope. Ultimately, all celebrations of the body must take place in the bones of history.

New York City, 1995

I Am

I am of the people who have no mythologies, no goddesses powerful and hidden, to call on. I am of the people who have no memories of other lands beneath their feet other than the cement slabs of city streets. I have no secret languages, no deeper words than the words I have learned in this world. I have no memory of fruits hanging, thick and full, of mountain tops and valleys marked by great happenings. I know no other rivers than the ones that bound my days on this city island. I do not mourn these losses because I cannot pretend I have lived where I have not. My memory cannot go back over long personal years. I do not know the name of my grandmother, so I am forced to go deep, diving through my own accumulated years to seize upon newly ancient fragments.

I have no other name than the one I carry. I know it only in one language. I hear no echoes when I say my name, a name of two words. The first commemorates my father, Jonas, whom I never knew; so does the second, my last name. I am named for a ghost. I am named for a heritage whose face I have never seen, whose voice I have never heard. Regina, my mother, lives nowhere in my name. I will not take her name to pull her into artificial life because the truth lies deeper. I must carry her in a different place, in a nameless place. She is not spirit but memory. She cannot be called forth by candles or by chants. She is now sights and sounds that lie on the floor of my memory. No litany of 'Regina, daughter of . . .' will put her back in time; there are too many missing names. The remembered click of her work heels in the hallway telling me she was returning home, and my happiness at that sound, must stand against eternity.

I have no rituals to call up lost worlds of power or of love. I wear no belly strings and carry no beads that stretch back into time and connect me to ancestors who sang at small altars. I am only here with a shallow pool of time around my toes. But that here has been my history. I stand in the dusk of a Manhattan day, the wind brisk and cold. I watch the bowed figures hurrying home, watch them step down from buses, lurch up from the subway, watch them head homeward with newspapers crushed under their arms, and I see a moment of human truth, the desire to rest after work, the need to be home. I stand knowing in my bones this city of tired workers. I have enough to cherish in just the courage of these days and nights. This is my land, my ancient totems, this tenacious grip on life.

This was written after having read 'My Last Name' by Nicolas Guillen, an Afro-Cuban poet, in *The Great Zoo and Other Poems*, translated by Robert Marquez (Monthly Review Press, New York, 1972).

Liberties Not Taken

Mac was a big man, a square-jawed engineer who built bridges and looked like he could shove them into place. He was laying stretched out on our couch with my mother sitting alongside him, as if he were ill. I could tell she was impressed that a person such as he – what she called a professional – was listening to her. Standing quietly before him, answering his questions and looking mainly at the soles of his shoes, I realized I had been summoned to pass some unknown test. His questions seemed to come from far away, and he barely moved his head to acknowledge that my voice was reaching him. I understood then that he was not ill, but that it was his power over us, the two women, that kept him so regally immobile. I did not know who he was or why he had this power, but I had learned by this, my thirteenth year (1953), that men were my mother's secret.

After the interrogation, he asked me if I would like to spend a summer in the country helping his wife Jean care for their five children, 'a mother's helper' he said. I knew then some of the talk that had gone on between the two of them: the sad tale of our circumstances, my mother's worry that I was getting into trouble. I had already been in a fight at school. Here was a chance for me to see what a real family was like. I accepted and prepared for a journey into other people's lives.

Early the next week, we left for the cottage in a battered blue station wagon. I was packed in among the twins and the older boy and could barely hold my own among the tumbling duffle bags filled with T-shirts and sneakers. Mac and Jean were invisible to me, and I was not sure how I could help make some order out of this family chaos. The house was flat with small rooms, musty and bare. Somehow it swallowed all of us up each night and then in the day turned us loose on its screened-in porch and shaded lake front.

The first day Jean and I were alone with the children, I learned quickly that she knew exactly what she wanted from me. I was to help with the cooking and cleaning, and in the afternoons watch the kids as they played on the lake's edge. All of this was told me in a quick crisp voice while she never took her eyes off me, and then she said, 'Want to swim?'

I followed her down to the lake, walking behind her tall lean body and quietly wondered at what was to come. She strode into the water, swam powerfully out to the floating raft, and ignoring the wooden ladder, hauled herself up. I was still knee-deep in the lake's shallows, frightened by the muddy bottom. This was the first time I had felt dying leaves, soft sticks, and small shelled creatures under my feet. I kept my eyes on her as she looked toward me, and then she walked across the raft until she was balanced on the extreme edge, facing the water. She raised her arms straight above her head, stood perfectly tall and still, a long unbroken line, and then almost too quick for me to be sure I had seen it, she sprang high up into the air and did a deep dive into the grey water. So clean, so sharp, so strong. I had never before seen a woman do such a thing, except for Esther Williams in the movies. I had known only the tired women of the cities, women who like my mother dragged their bodies to work, stuffed them into too-tight shoes and full-line bras. I knew women's bodies were for sex, but I did not know they could cut through the water or leap straight up into the air. Jean surfaced not far from me, waved me on, and then walked quickly out of the water up the hill and back to the house. I stood silently, knowing I had seen a wonderful thing, knowing that a woman brave enough to do that was going to teach me things I would never forget.

As the days went by, I washed the dishes, cleaned the little square rooms, tended the four boys and the little girl who all had a California enthusiasm for the outdoors that left me exhausted, and most of all, listened to Jean talk. I learned that she had met Mac when she was in the WAVES and he was in the Navy. Even after their marriage, her favorite nights out were with her women buddies, spending long weekends in San Francisco bars. She had a special girlfriend, a woman who delighted in dropping her glass eye into her Scotch and watching other patrons turn away in disgust. The eye would sit there in the amber water, staring up at them as the evening wore on. Eventually Mac would storm into the place, drag Jean out, and fuck her hard that night as if he could drive their deep women's laughter out of her belly. But Jean would keep returning to the bars and to her one special friend. Five children later, to save her from herself, Mac got a new job in New York, moved the family, and for a short time ended up in the same square desolate housing development as we had.

She told me these things as if I would understand them and I did. She taught me to play poker and got angry when I made a mistake, but it was anger that made me feel proud. She let me drive the car down the dirt roads, and one night she took me to a drive-in and let me lie with my head in her lap and dangle my feet out of the window. She made me laugh until I couldn't stop and looking down at me, she started laughing too. I felt it deep in her bones; she had no belly, just taut skin stretched over her bones. My head rolled with her laughter. Then I felt her hands on my face, on my hair, and a sweetness overcame me. I wanted never to take my head out of her lap, wanted her laughter pouring out over me for always because with it came a caring and an indulgence too sweet, too grand to let time take away.

She introduced me to her gay nephew who visited irregularly throughout the summer. Mac hated this young man who wore his suit jacket over his shoulders, smelled of perfume, and read Anais Nin. She arranged a date between us, and we sat in the borrowed car for a respectable amount of time before returning, aware that we were thrown together for a purpose but not yet having words to share our longings. I didn't call myself gay yet. For three years I had been making love to my best friend Roz Rabinowitz with my mouth, and I knew the word *Lesbian*, but I was terrified of its implications and could not say it.

With Jean it was different; I was not afraid of being anything she was – except Mac's wife. We spent the long weekday nights playing cards with the older women who shared a cabin down the road. Every night before we went to bed she asked me to massage her back. I would straddle her, marveling at her body that was her ally, the muscles lying lean on the bones. I longed to slip my hands around her, to catch her small pointed breasts in my hands, to extend the travel of my fingers down the small of her back to her buttocks, to slip gently into her, and to give her all the pleasure there was in my thirteen-year-old imagination to give. I wanted to lie beside her, hoping that she would wrap her long legs around me and carry me with her in her leaps for freedom. I never had the courage to do these things. I just whispered 'I love you', as she stretched under my hands.

When Mac arrived for the weekends, they would move into the double bed on the porch, and I would hear their arguments, hear Jean saying, 'I don't want to, leave me alone.' Then I would hear her being fucked, a hard rushing sound that silenced her. I wondered where the strength went that I saw all week until I pictured Mac, a huge man who was sure he knew what was good for her.

One weekend after they had fought particularly hard, we were all in the lake together. I was out over my head, but I wasn't afraid because Jean was there. All of a sudden Mac, whose head was only a few feet away from me, said, 'You have never been kissed by a father. I will show you what it is like.' And he swam toward me, a large moving head with an open mouth and a power hidden beneath the surface. I tried to swim to land, but he grabbed me and held my head while he pushed his tongue deep into my mouth. I churned my arms and legs to keep from drowning, and finally he let me go. I swam desperately for shore, not wanting to see Jean's face, not wanting to see her failure.

I had been kissed like this before, by the lonely fireman whose wife had just brought home their new baby. While she was upstairs showing it off to the other little girls, he sat beside me on the sofa, showing me a picture of a naked Hawaiian woman. Then he kissed me, pushed his tongue into my mouth. I was ten years old. And two years later, my mother's lover forcing me to give him a 'real kiss goodnight', the same tongue this time joined with a knee between my twelve-year-old legs and his hand squeezing my breasts. And it was to happen many years later when a renowned young doctor kissed me in front of my woman lover to show me what I really needed. Always it was done to save me, to show me something I did not know, and always it resulted in near drowning. It was not that I lacked desire; I longed for Jean's lips. But because I did not tell her clearly that it was my yearning, my choice, my passion that wanted her, a thirteen-year-old knowledge that was deep and fine, she and I did nothing, and Mac kissed me and fucked her.

As the summer wore on, Jean gave me more freedom from my chores, and I made friends with the teenage counselors who worked in the Jewish socialist camp a few yards down the beach. I quickly found myself in their world of summer camp romances. The summer was dying and Stanley, the City College freshman who had become my half-hearted pursuer, convinced me to have a party on the beach near our cabin. It started late, a late summer night, a night of teenage scents – beer, cigarettes, Scotch – of wet kisses, fumblings, twistings in the blankets, the fire blazing up; couples, the young men laying on the young women, rubbing their swollen needs. I did not want it and retreated from my young man to sit in the gently rocking canoe, knowing the summer was going to end and wondering if my deliverance would come. He followed me, angry that I had deserted our chance to open mouths to each other. I sat still in the night air, seeing his lips move but not hearing his words.

My whole body was tuned for another sound. I knew she

would come, and I wanted to show her I recognized my difference. I will bide my time until she touches me. I want her hands on me, her tongue in my mouth. I want to hold her head against me and throw my legs around her. And then I heard her canoe coming, the slow dipping of the paddle. I saw her flashlight search for me among the coupled bodies. Sooner than I thought possible she shone the light full on me, her eyes dark in her small face. The others in the canoe sat in the shadows behind her, but she forgot they were there. I answered her before she spoke. 'I am here. I am only talking, waiting.'

'I would have killed you if you were there,' she said, flashing her light over the entangled bodies as if she were a general surveying a field of fallen opponents.

No, Jean. You gave me the freedom to choose, but you feared that freedom more than you knew. I showed you in the best way I could that it was your touch I sought, and in the end all you could give me was the suspicion that I had not listened, had not heard your stories, not recognized your gifts of woman difference. You heard their voices, not mine, because I was a girl-woman and it was a dangerous thing to touch me, and yet I had been touched so many times before by men who did not pause to think of innocence. Your touch would have healed me. But we had been judged unclean, and you would not harm me with the power of what they called our sin.

The summer ended. My mother lost the apartment, and I went back to live with my childless aunt and uncle in their grey rooms. I never saw Jean again, but my mother must have because she told me five years later that Jean was dead of breast cancer. My high deep diver, I would have touched you so.

The Killing Air

1943:

A strong blond man held me in his arms, my short skirt lapping over his muscles. My mother stood beside him, looking up at me. With his free hand, he was pulling the Bronx curtain shut. A blackout, my mother said. So the enemy planes can't see our lights.

1945:

I was home alone, sitting on the living room floor, playing with the encyclopedia volumes my mother had bought from a man who came to the door. I had made a many-leveled fort out of the big dark-blue squares and peopled them with pennies, standing on their edges as sentinels. Soon I became aware of a low wailing sound filling the room along with the rays of sunshine that shone on the wooden floor. I ran to the window and looked up and down the street. Then I realized that the sound was coming from other open windows all around me. Women, their heads covered with aprons, were weeping at the windows, some crying out, 'Our President is dead, he is dead.' All up and down Gun Hill Road, women were keening their loss. I stared, wondering how this death, this sorrow, had made its way into Bronx kitchens smelling from chickens and onions.

1949:

Mrs Worthy stood in front of her desk, a signal to us all that she was going to say something very important. She put her hands behind her and leaned her upper body into us. 'Now children, you remember how I have been telling you about the isms that are America's danger.' We all nodded. How could we forget the weekly reading Mrs Worthy made us endure from a book she obviously thought was a bible for the times. Her favorite sermons were on the danger of communism, the ism that made her blue-white hair get even bluer and her voice grow deep with sternness. 'This is National Negro Week, and you all have to write an essay on a famous American Negro. But children,' she leaned even closer, 'there is one man you must not write about. He is a disgrace to this country.' I twisted in my seat. 'His name is Paul Robeson, and he is a communist.' The anger and contempt in her voice were too big for this fourth-grade class.

Mrs Worthy was our social studies teacher, and she had already taught me more than she would ever know. Earlier in the year she had been lecturing us, once again, on the evils that plagued this country. Only this time her subject was key children. The trouble with this country, she confided to us, were those key children, those wild children left free to roam the streets by uncaring mothers. These dirty and disrespectful children were lowering the standards of our country. I tried to sink into my seat because I was one of those latchkey children and as she spoke the metal key around my neck began to burn into my flesh. Slowly, slowly I inched my hand up to my chest and quickly tucked the hated emblem into my sweater. I had already known I was different. I had no father; my mother worked. But I had not known I was a national disgrace. Along with the shame of that day, however, I learned something else: authority often said things that were not true about people it did not know, that enemies were made of those who were different, and that I would struggle never to accept dictated hatreds.

When Mrs Worthy said Paul Robeson was an enemy, I immediately knew I had to find out who he was and write about him. After school, I anxiously waited for my mother to come home so I could ask her about this man. A great man, she said, who believed in peace. I spent the next few days finding out all I could about him and wrote an essay called, 'Paul Robeson: A Great American.' Although Mrs Worthy never spoke to me about it, I had won two gifts for myself: a lifelong appreciation for Paul Robeson's spirit and the knowledge that ideas passionately lived in the world. If I had accepted the voice of orthodoxy in this early skirmish with McCarthy America, I would never have found the courage to claim my Lesbian life ten years later.

1953–1959:

In the year 1953, I was thirteen years old and newly settled with an aunt and uncle in Bayside, Queens. All of Bayside seemed new then, streets without sidewalks, roped-off lots on which houses were to bloom, and always the ubiquitous housing developments managing to look worn even in their infancy. Working people lived in these small red squares, lured from the older boroughs to new homesteads awaiting them at the end of endless subway and bus rides. New institutions had to be built to serve the children of these seduced pilgrims, and Martin Van Buren High School was one of them. Constructed to house the overflow from older schools like Jamaica and Bayside High, it lay squat and sprawling along the turnpike. Here, in these new halls, I met Susan Bender who was to teach me so much. She was an awkward, square, thin young woman who put her hair in the demanded ponytail, but in no other way did she adhere to the fashions of her times. She wore long brown skirts, white socks and moccasins, and walked with her shoulders first. She was open and friendly and alone. She and her mother and father lived across from the luncheonette, another artifact, in one of the first red brick developments.

Susan attracted me. I thought she was butchy and I sensed a strong body under her unattractive clothes. I was looking for this secret strength even then. I remember one afternoon trying to seduce her in her bedroom, and somehow handcuffs were a part of the game. I soon realized, however, that even though Susan looked the part, she was slow to follow my lead. Appearance was not always the same as potential, I had to learn grudgingly.

Disappointed with how Susan was adhering to her wholesome school-girlishness, I went downstairs to visit with her mother. She seemed pleased that Susan had a friend. We sat outside on two small concrete steps, and she gave me a cup of tea. Flattered by the attention of this older, kind woman, I searched for something mature to say. A vague memory of Susan saying her parents were radical popped into my mind, and at the same time words that were all around me came from my lips. I said something about how Communists were turning up everywhere. Then I sat back to watch this woman run, and she did. Her whole demeanor changed. I was looking straight ahead at the spotty earth that passed for a back yard, but I was aware of her every movement. Before my words, spoken just to test their power, we had been comrades sitting comfortably side by side on raw cement steps. Afterward, she stopped speaking, drew her hunched shoulders up, and gave a long, deep sigh, as if I had disappointed her terribly. Then, in one continuous move, she got up and disappeared into the house. I never spoke to her again.

I sat alone, knowing exactly what I had done. I had played with her, sensing she was a hunted person, a ready-made victim for me if I only said the right words, if I hinted I knew her secret. I, a young girl, had overturned her world. This was the power that floated in the air; anyone could use it. Malice, carelessness, ignorance could pluck hate from the air and hurl it at a human target. As I sat there, alone, I felt the weight of her absence. I needed friends as much as Susan did; I needed a mother even more. And yet here, through a calculated manipulation of words, I had destroyed a moment of human solidarity. I had felt like an outcast for so long myself that I had risen to the bait of making someone else more uncomfortable than I was. I hated myself at that moment, but I had learned another searing lesson: politics, the battle over ideas going on all around me, was not an abstract discussion but a weapon aimed at a people's heart, and for one moment I had held the weapon.

Susan's mother obviously did not tell her daughter what had happened because a few months later Susan called me, all excited. Did I want to go see the Bolshoi Ballet with her? It was their first appearance in America. Now, I had never been to any ballet and I had no idea who the Bolshoi was. She explained it was the Russian national ballet company. The excitement in Susan's voice and the dreariness of my foster home pushed me to say yes. We would have to stand on the line for hours, even for whole days, to get a standing-room ticket, Susan warned. We planned to meet at the bus stop the next day.

For the following two weeks, everything else vanished: school, other friends, my aunt and uncle. I lived for the glory Susan had brought me. Every day we would meet, wearing our line clothes: for me, a shirtwaist paisley dress and sneakers; for Susan, her ever-present brown skirt and white socks with loafers. I never changed my outfit. It was the only dress I had, and it ate up the stains of the sidewalk – the dribbled coffee, the bits of tuna fish. And always there was the lunch that Susan's mother had packed. She was with us.

Early in the morning we would get our place in line, over the days getting to know our comrades who stood shivering in the cold morning air with us. We huddled against the wall, sat on the street when the sun came out, took turns running for coffee or going to pee in friendly restaurants. The street became our living room; we knew every crack, every inch of the long block. We minutely discussed the performance we had seen the night before, and I heard myself using words I had just learned: her points were wonderful, his leaps were so athletic. Russian names, garbled but adored, poured out of me – Plisetskaya, Ulanova. Like the young boy in 'Paul's Case', I had found a world of romance and wonder, a place where ugliness and loneliness had been replaced by shattering beauty and the glory of human accomplishment.

We were always the youngest people on the line and certainly the least knowledgeable, but by the sixth day, we were accepted by the aging ballet students, the retired dancers, the devotees of Russian culture who packed the line. Some-times, if we were lucky, the Russian dancers would come out for a stroll in the afternoon sun, and we would see them laughing like real people, the men wearing their jackets draped over their shoulders, the women smaller than they appeared on stage, disappearing into their furs.

Then, as the sky darkened, we would be given our numbers guaranteeing us a place among the elect for the evening's performance. Once inside, we huddled twenty deep along the side walls, held back by a thick maroon rope from the aristocratic crowds that poured down the orchestra aisles every night. Never had I been so close to wealth and to the famous. But vastly more important, never had I been part of an artistic world, never had I seen the beauty of movement and heard the splendor of music that I was witnessing because Susan had called me.

The wonder of the dances overpowered everything else. When the lights fell and the surging music began, I cared nothing for what was around me or what it all meant. I only knew that Plisetskaya was dying, that her arms were the hurt wings of a gentle swan, and that the music was soothing every wound I had. I accepted the tale of Giselle, the peasant girl who goes crazy and dances with ghosts. Night after night, dancer after dancer carried me into the peasant's painted cottage, into the dream world of the second act where ghostlike maidens danced a poignant welcome to the lost lover. The Bronx where I had been born, the mother that I had to leave to live, all retreated before the power of the dancer and the music. Surely I could believe in the transformation of lovers into swans: was I not transformed by this nightly spectacle?

I saw men with muscled thighs throw themselves toward the dark heavens of the theater and return to earth only to soar again. Then one night I saw something else. During one of the elaborate ballroom scenes when the whole corps was on stage, one of the specialty dancers came to the front of the stage to do his famous leap. A small man, dressed in a jester's suit, he was well known to the audience. The music swelled, and the dancer began his preparations for his famous leap. He soared high off the stage with the audience beginning to applaud wildly, but when he landed, he lost his balance and fell. The audience held its breath. He carefully got up, motioned to the conductor, and the same music began again. Once again he prepared himself and leaped even higher. This time his small whirling body landed perfectly poised, and everyone on the stage and in the audience roared their respect. I had never before seen the dignity of artistic failure, the dedication to accomplishment that outweighed the nightmare of humiliation. I thought then that I had looked into the Russian soul; now I think it was the soul of an artist.

At the end of each night's performance, a ritual of exuberant mutual appreciation took place. The audience would rush toward the stage, throwing single roses and shouting out the names of their favorite dancers. The dancers approached as close to the end of the stage as they dared and stood clapping their outstretched hands. We learned to shout *spasibo*, the Russian word for thank you. Whenever I said it, I felt as if I had traveled around the world, as if I had left the America of the fifties far behind me.

After the performances, Susan and I would attach ourselves to a group of older and wiser standees who gathered in an all-night automat to savour the performance. We never asked permission to come along: we just followed the group, knowing our place of respectful silence. We would sit at the end of the table, coffee and donuts in front of us, drinking up their dedication. These were not fashionable people. They looked poor and rumpled, but they were at the heart of what we were experiencing. An older Black woman, her hair pulled tightly back into a bun, was the leading figure in the group. She strongly but lovingly pointed out all the faults and wonders of the performances. Gesturing with long thin fingers, she compared Plisetskaya's moves to those of another dancer that we did not know. French words, technical terms, shouts of disagreement flowed across the table. Hour after hour the dance went on.

Susan and I would ride the subway late at night, exhausted, blissful, back to the barrenness of Bayside. One night as we were half-asleep on the train, I took out of the pocket of my dress, which was creased and dirty from the days on the sidewalk, a few crumbs of bread and held them in the palm of my hand for Susan to see. An old woman sitting across from us got up, lurched across the aisle, and put a dollar in my outstretched hand. I couldn't understand and tried to return it to her, but she just kept shaking her head no, gesturing with her hand, that I should keep it. I realized what I must have looked like. Dirty, hair wild, torn sneakers, a handful of crumbs. But my eyes, they were shining, my heart was full of richness. I had been in another world far from the greyness of my youth. I had been with people who had a passion, a discipline. I had spoken a foreign word in a forbidden tongue. I had found another air to breathe.

A Restricted Country

1.

When the plane landed on the blazing tar strip, I knew Arizona was a new world. My mother and brother stared with me out at the mountain-fringed field of blue. The Nestles three on their first vacation together had crossed the Mississippi and entered the shining new land of the American West. The desert air hit us with its startling clarity: this was not the intimate heat of New York, the heat that penetrated flesh and transformed itself into our sweat and earned our curses. We walked through it, like the others, and stood waiting for the station wagon to pick us up.

I should have known from the skeptical look on my mother's face that we were in for trouble, but I chalked it up to the fact that she had never traveled further west than New Jersey. My brother's new job at American Airlines had made this trip possible: the company compensated for low wages by offering its employees special cut-rate vacation packages, and many of his fellow workers had recommended this one-week stay at Shining Star Guest Ranch as the best bargain. From the moment he had told us of the possibility, to the time we were standing in front of the Tucson Airport, I could not believe the trip was really going to happen. I had dreamed horses all my sixteen years, played wild stallion in the Bronx vacant lots that were my childhood fields, had read every book about wild

horses, mustangs, rangy colts that I could find, and through all
the splintering agonies of my family I galloped on plains that
were smooth and never-ending. For my brother, who had
seldom been with my mother and me, this trip was both a
reunion and an offering. After years of turmoil, mistakes and
rage, he was giving us the spoils of his manhood. He lay this
vacation at the feet of our fatherless family as if it were a long-
awaited homecoming gift. For my mother, it was a simple
thing: her week's vacation from the office, her first trip in over
twenty years.

We finally spotted the deep-purple station wagon that bore
the ranch's name and hurried to it. A large man in a cowboy hat
asked if we were the Nestle family, looked at us intently, and
then fell silent as he loaded our suitcases into the wagon. We
rode through the outskirts of Tucson and continued into the
desert. The man never said another word to us, and feeling the
strangeness of the desert, we too fell silent. Cacti rose around
us, twisted strong creatures that, like the untouching heat,
seemed only to tolerate the temporary intrusion of roads into
their world. I felt the desert clumps of tufted grass under my
feet. I was already moving my horse's haunches, for now it was
only a sheet of glass that separated me from Annie Oakley.
Dusk came suddenly and the heat fled.

We pulled into the ranch, and another man poked his head
into the front window and stared at the three of us. 'Do you
want fish or meat for dinner?' were his only words. My mother
answered that it made no difference, meat would be fine.
Everything was still in the blue-black night as we were shown
our rooms and then led to the dining room. The room was long,
low-roofed with heavy beams; a fireplace glowed at one end. All
the other guests were seated at the same table, ladling out huge
portions of food from communal platters. We were seated at the
long last table, a far distance from the rest, near the large stone
fireplace. As our places were being set, the waitress placed a
small white card near each of our plates. I picked up mine
and read, *Because this guest ranch is run like a family, we are
restricted to members of the Gentile faith only.* I could now

envision the chain of events that our arrival had set in motion. The man who peered in at us must have realized we were Jewish, rushed in to tell his boss, who pulled out the appropriate cards to be served with our dinner. My brother and I sat stunned; my mother said we would talk to the manager after dinner.

As I tried to eat, the voices of the other guests caught in my throat. I had grown up with the language of New York's garment district. I knew the word *goy*, but this was my introduction to *Gentiles*. We can't stay here, my mother said. My brother kept saying he was sorry, he didn't know. How could his coworkers recommend this place? How could American Airlines have a working agreement with such a place? When we finished eating, my mother asked to speak to the manager. She and my brother were led to his office. I stayed outside in what seemed to be a reading room. I paced the room, looking at the books lining the wall. Finally, I found what I knew had to be there: a finely bound volume of *Mein Kampf*. For one moment it wasn't 1956 but another time, a time of flaming torches and forced marches. It wasn't just my Jewishness that I learned at that moment: it was also the stunning reality of exclusion unto death. It was the history lesson of those judged not to be human, and I knew our number was legion and so were our dyings.

Huddled in the privacy of our room, my mother and brother told me what the manager had said. Since it was off-season, he was willing to compromise. If we told no one that we were Jewish, if we left and entered through the back door, and if we ate our meals by ourselves, we could stay. We looked at each other. Here was an offer to the Nestles to pass as Gentiles. To eat and walk in shame.

We waited until the morning to tell the manager our decision. I stayed in our room while my mother and brother went in for breakfast. In a strange twist of feeling, my anger had turned to shyness. I thought of the priest I had noticed sitting at the table the night before, and I could not bear the thought of making him see we were human. I could not bear the challenge to his geniality that we would represent. After breakfast, the three of us entered the manager's office to tell him we would not stay under his conditions.

I stared at the man as my mother spoke for us, looking for his embarrassment, waiting for the moment when he would say this was all a joke. His answer was that he was sure we would not want to stay some place we were not wanted, but there was a Jewish dude ranch several miles away. Perhaps the owners would consider allowing us to stay there for the same price. He made the call for us, saying, 'By mistake some of your people came here.' The voice on the other end agreed to take us. Once again we were ushered into the station wagon and driven to a parking lot in downtown Tucson. We sat on the curb waiting for the new station wagon to pick us up. The men walking by wore big brown belts with turquoise stones embedded in the leather, pointed boots, and wide-brimmed hats. The sun shone with that same impersonal heat, and the shimmering mountains were still waiting for us in the distance.

2.

When the station wagon pulled into our new destination, we were greeted by a small circle of elderly guests who welcomed us with hugs and low-voiced comments to my mother about 'the *kinder*'. After the novelty of our sad mistake wore off, the three of us were left to our own devices. As the youngest person at the ranch, I was indulged in my unladylike ways. Riding clothes were lent to me, and my desire to smell as much like a horse as possible was humorously accepted. My brother spent his time playing tennis and dating a young woman who cleaned the rooms. As soon as it grew dark, they would take off for the nearest town. My mother, however, had a harder time in our Jewish haven. All the other guests were retired, wealthy married couples who moved with ease in this sunlit world. While they were sympathetic to my mother, a woman alone raising two kids, they were also embarrassed by her. She dressed wrong and did not know how to enjoy herself.

My mother was a dedicated gin and poker player. Shortly after our arrival she tried to join the nightly card game, but here, under the Arizona sun, the stakes had multiplied beyond her resources. I watched her as she approached the table of cigar-smoking men. She sat for one round, growing smaller in her seat while the pile of chips grew bigger and bigger in the center of the table. She was a working-class gambler who played with her week's salary while these men played with their retired riches. Her Seventh Avenue bravado could not cover her cards. For the first time in my life, I saw my mother defeated by the people she said she despised. She could not fight the combination of a strange country, high fashion, pity, money, and physical pride.

One afternoon I noticed a crowd of guests gesturing and laughing at something in the center of the riding ring. I pushed through and saw it was my mother. Dressed in her checked polyester suit, she sat on top of a large brown gelding attempting to move it. She rocked back and forth in the saddle as if she were on a rocking horse, or making love, while voices cried out to her, 'Come on, Regina, kick him. You can do it.' The intimate spectacle of my mother's awkwardness, the one-sided laughter, and the desperate look on her face pushed me back from the railing. These people were my people; they had been kind to me. But something terrible was going on here. We were Jewish, but we were different.

Toward evening, at the end of our stay, I went in search of my mother. I looked by the pool, in the lounge, and everywhere else the other guests habitually gathered, but I could not find her. I wandered to the far end of the ranch and saw her in the distance. She was sitting on a child's swing, trailing one leg in the dust. A small round woman whose belly bulged in her too-tight, too-cheap pants. Her head was lowered, and the air shimmered around her as if loneliness had turned to heat. Where was Seventh Avenue, the coffee shops, the crowded subways, the city which covered her aloneness because she had work to do there. Arizona was not for Regina Nestle, not this resort with its well-married ladies. While I scrambled over this new brown earth, my mother sat in the desert, a silent exile.

3.

Bill, the tired, aging cowboy who ran the corral, was my date for the evening. Elliot was with Mary, a woman in her twenties who worked at the ranch. We had been to see a movie and were now parked behind the ranch house. Bill kissed me as we twisted around in the front seat. His bony hand pushed into my crotch while his tongue opened my mouth. I pushed his hand away, sure of what I wanted and of what I did not. I did not want his fingers in me, but I did want so see his cheek against my breast. My brother and Mary gave up their squirming in the back seat and left the two of us alone. Bill was respectful. One word from me was enough to get him to stop his attempts at penetration. 'Lay in my arms,' I told him. He slipped his long legs through the open window at one end of the front seat and leaned back into my arms. His lips pulled at my nipples. We sat that way for a long time as the Arizona sky grew darker and darker. Right before he fell asleep, he said, 'Best thing that's happened to me in twenty years.' I knew this did not have very much to do with me, but a lot to do with my sixteen-year-old breasts. I sat there holding him for what seemed like hours, afraid to move because I did not want to wake him, when suddenly he jerked in his sleep and knocked into the steering wheel, setting off the horn. The desert stillness was split by its harsh alarm, and I knew my idyll was coming to an end.

One by one, the lights came on in the guest cottages. My brother was the first to reach the car, his pajamas shining white in the moonlight. 'I'm alright, I'm alright,' I whispered, as I maneuvered my body away from Bill's. I wanted to escape before the other guests came pouring out, to save Bill from having to explain what we were doing. He would be held responsible for breaking the boundaries between guests and workers, between young girls and old men, and I would never be able to convince them that I knew exactly what I was doing, that tenderness was my joy that night, that I danced in the moonlight knowing my body could be a home in the freezing desert air.

4.

I spent most of my time around the horses, following Bill on his daily chores. He eventually gave me his chaps to wear because I was constantly riding into the cholla plants and ending up with their needles sticking into my thighs. My horse for the week was not the sleek stallion I had dreamed of, but a fat wide-backed white mare that was safe. Ruby and I were always on the tail end of the rides, but I did not care: the Bronx streets had disappeared, and I could bend over and talk to my steed while I stroked her powerful neck.

Each day we rode up into the mountains, the same mountains that had looked so distant from the airport. Our party was usually Elliot and myself, and Bill and Elizabeth. Elizabeth was a small muscular woman in her fifties whose husband was dying of Parkinson's disease. She had made my riding possible by lending me a pair of boots. Each morning her husband, a large burly man who walked in tiny trembling steps, would stand in the doorway of their cottage and slowly raise his hand to wave good-bye. Elizabeth loved him deeply, and each morning I saw the grief on her face. She would ride her horse like a demon far up into the mountains, leaving the rest of us behind. As the week passed, I slowly realized that she and Bill were lovers. I saw the tenderness between them as if it were an invisible rope that kept them both from falling off the rocky hills. Like two aging warriors, both grey and lean, they fought off sadness with sharp, quick actions. We would ride up into the mountain clefts, find a grassy spot to stretch out on in the afternoon sun, and silently be glad for each other's company. I never spoke or intruded on their moments together. I just watched and learned from their sad, tough, erotic connection all I could bear about illness and love and sexuality. On the way home, stumbling down the stony trails, I would ride as close as I could to these two silent adults.

Then it was our last ride together. We had come down from the mountains on a different path. We found a dirt road, smooth enough for cars, and I started to see real estate signs announcing that this area was the most restricted country in Arizona. I pushed my horse closer to Elizabeth and Bill and asked, 'What does *restricted* mean?'

'No Jews allowed,' Elizabeth answered. I looked around again in wonder at this land we were moving through. The distant hills had become known, and I loved this earth so different from my own. I silently rode beside my two older friends, wanting to be protected by their gentle toughness and not understanding how the beauty of the land could be owned by ugliness.

The Bathroom Line
Dedicated to the Lesbians of the Fifties

We had rituals too, back in the old days, rituals born
out of our Lesbian time and place, the geography of the fifties.
The Sea Colony* was a world of ritual display – deep dances of
Lesbian want, Lesbian adventuring, Lesbian bonding. We who
lived there knew the steps. It was over twenty-five years ago,
but I can still peer into the smoke-filled room, feel the pressure
of bodies, look for the wanted face to float up out of the haze
into the circle of light, the tumult of recognition. 'I wondered
how long it would take you to come here,' the teacher
welcomes her adoring student, and then retreats into the
womanmade mist.

Because we lived in the underworld of the Sea Colony, we
were surrounded by the nets of the society that hated us and
yet wanted our money. Mafia nets, clean-up New York nets,
vice squad nets. We needed the Lesbian air of the Sea Colony to
breathe the life we could not anywhere else, those of us who
wanted to see women dance, make love, wear shirts and pants.
Here, and in other bars like this one, we found each other and
the space to be a sexually powerful butch-femme community.
We entered their nets with rage, with need and with strength.
The physical nets were visible, and we knew how to side-step
them, to slip by, just as we knew, holding hands in the street,
clear butch-femme couples, which groups of straights to stay

* The Sea Colony was a working-class Lesbian bar in New York City. I was part of
its world from 1958 until the mid-sixties.

away from, which cars flashed danger as they slowed down at the corner of the curb. We knew how to move quickly. We had the images of smashed faces clear in our memories: our lovers, our friends who had not moved quickly enough. It was the other nets, the nets of the righteous people, the ones that reached into our minds, that most threatened our breathing. These nets carried twisted in their invisible windings the words *hate yourself because you are a freak, hate yourself because you use your tongue, hate yourself because you look butch and femme, hate yourself because you are sexual.*

The powers of the mainland controlled our world in some obvious ways. The cops would come in to check their nets, get their payoffs, joke with the men who stood by the door. They would poke their heads into the back room to make sure we were not dancing together, a crime for which we could be arrested. Of course, the manager had flashed the red light ten minutes before the cops arrived to warn us to play our parts. We did, sitting quietly at the square tables as the cops looked us over. But if they had looked closer, they would have seen hands clenched under the tables, femmes holding on to the belts of their butches, saying through the touch of fingers: don't let their power, their swagger, their leer, goad you into battle. We will lose, and they will take pleasure in our pain, in our blood.

But the most searing reminder of our colonized world was the bathroom line. Now I know it stands for all the pain and glory of my time, and I carry that line and the women who endured it deep within me. Because we were labeled deviants, our bathroom habits had to be watched. Only one woman at a time was allowed into the toilet because we could not be trusted. Thus the toilet line was born, a twisting horizon of Lesbian women waiting for permission to urinate, to shit.

The line flowed past the far wall, past the bar, the front room tables, and reached into the back room. Guarding the entrance to the toilet was a short, square, handsome butch woman, the same every night, whose job it was to twist around her hand our allotted amount of toilet paper. She was us, an obscenity, doing the man's tricks so we could breathe. The line awaited all of us every night, and we developed a line act. We joked, we cruised, we commented on the length of time one of us took, we made special pleas to allow hot-and-heavy lovers in together, knowing full well that our lady would not permit it. I stood, a femme, loving the women on either side of me, loving my comrades for their style, the power of their stance, the hair hitting the collar, the thrown-out hip, the hand encircling the beer can. Our eyes played the line, subtle touches, gentle shyness weaved under the blaring jokes, the music, the surveillance. We lived on that line; restricted and judged, we took deep breaths and played.

But buried deep in our endurance was our fury. That line was practice and theory seared into one. We wove our freedoms, our culture, around their obstacles of hatred, but we also paid our price. Every time I took the fistful of toilet paper, I swore eventual liberation. It would be, however, liberation with a memory.

Esther's Story

I had heard of Esther. She was tough, a passing*
woman whose lover was a prostitute. Sea Colony talk. We all
knew stories about each other, but like huge ice floes, we
could occupy the same ocean without touching. This night we
touched. She was sitting at the bar speaking a soft Spanish to
Maria, the bartender from Barcelona. Amidst the noise and
smoke, Esther sat straight and still, a small slim woman who
dressed butch. Her profile was severe, grey hair rising from her
forehead and waving back in the classic DA style. A small mole
broke the tautness of her face. I do not remember how our
contact began, but at some point I was standing between her
legs as she sat with the lights of the bar at her back. Her knees
jutted out around me like a sharp cove on a rocky shore. She
joked with me, and I worried that I could not hold her attention.
I was not sure I wanted to. We were wary of each other, but an
erotic need had flashed between us, and neither of us would let
it go.

Later that night she offered to take me home. We agreed to
go for a drive first. The night was dark, and Esther drove with
ease, one hand on the wheel, the other holding her endless
cigarette. She told me how she had left Ponce, Puerto Rico, her

*The word *passing* is used here to represent a Lesbian who looked like a man to
the straight world. She wore men's clothes and worked at what was considered a
man's job, such as driving a taxi or clerking in a stockroom. Language here is
inadequate, however. Neither *passing* nor *transvestism* explains the experience
of the passing woman. Only she can.

grown sons, and her merchant sailor husband, to come to America to live like she wanted. Her family had cursed her, and she had built a new family here in New York. Her life was hard. Her girlfriend gave her a lot of trouble; they both had struggled with drugs, but life was getting better now. She enjoyed driving the taxi, and because her customers thought she was a man, they never bothered her. I looked at her, at the woman in a neat white shirt and grey pants, and wondered how her passengers could be so deceived. It was our womanness that rode with us in the car, that filled the night with tense possibilities.

Our ride ended in a vast parking lot at Jones Beach. Spotted around the lot were other cars, far enough away from each other so that lovers could have privacy. We sat in silence for a while, with Esther's cigarette a sharp red circle moving in the car's darkness. She put out the light and turned toward me. I leaned into her, fearing her knowledge, her toughness – and then I realized her hands were trembling. Through my blouse, I could feel her hands like butterflies shaking with respect and need. Younger lovers had been harder, more toughened to the joy of touch, but my passing woman trembled with her gentleness. I opened to her, wanting to wrap my fuller body around her leanness. She was pared down for battle, but in the privacy of our passion she was soft and careful. We kissed for a long time. I pressed my breasts hard into her, wanting her to know that even though I was young, I knew the strength of our need, that I was swollen with it. Finally she pulled away, and we started the long drive home. She asked me if she could spend the night. I said no, because I had to get up to go to work in a couple of hours and because I could no longer balance my need for Esther and the fear that I was beginning something I could not control. She said she would call. She told me later that I was the first woman who had said no to her. She said it with admiration, and I felt dishonest. It was not femme purity that kept me from her that night.

A few weeks passed, and I was sitting in the back room of the Sea Colony waiting for Vicki to return from cruising in the front room. A Seven-and-Seven appeared on the table.

'Compliments of her,' the waitress said, gesturing to the corner. I turned to see Esther smile, constrained but amused. Later in the night, when all things were foggier, I heard a whisper in my ear, 'You will be mine.' I just saw the shadow of her face before she disappeared.

She called not long after, and I invited her to dinner. I knew I was testing my boundaries, and I think she was too. I was a young femme seeking the response of women I adored, needing their desire deep inside of me. I had brought several women home to my railroad apartment on East Ninth Street, but usually I was in control: I was sexually more expressive and on my own territory. From the first with Esther, I knew it would be different. I was twenty, and she was forty-five. I was out only two years, and she had already lived lifetimes as a freak. Her sexuality was a world of developed caring, and she had paid a dear price for daring to be as clearly defined as she was.

The day of our dinner dragged at work. I knew I would not have time to change from work clothes and cook dinner before she arrived. At least that was my excuse for staying in my heels, nylons, and dress. But the deeper reason was that I wanted her to see my competent femme self, self-supporting and sturdy, and then I wanted her to reach under my dress, to penetrate the disguise I wore in a world that saw me as having no sexuality because I had neither boyfriend nor husband.

I bought a steak and mushrooms on the way home, prepared a big salad, and set the oval table in the third room, the combined living and bedroom. This was a scene I had prepared many times before, my foreplay of giving. Each time I had felt fear and pride that two women could dare each other so. At seven-thirty she knocked. I opened the door breathlessly, as if I had run a long way. She walked past me and stood in the center of the living room, looking around, while I explained that I had not had time to change. She was wearing a white-on-white shirt with ruffles down the front, sharply creased black pants, and loafers. Her slimness shone clean and sharp. All of a sudden I felt everything in the apartment was too big: I was too big, the table was too full, my need was too big. Esther stood quietly, looking at the set table filled with my offerings.

'Can't I do something for you please,' she said. She examined the old apartment until she found a chair that needed fixing. 'I'll fix that for you.'

'No, no please, you don't have to.'

'I want to.'

She left and returned in a few minutes with some tools. She turned the chair upside down and repaired it. Only then would she allow herself to sit at my table. 'So much food.' We both ate very little, weighed down by the erotic tension in the room.

After dinner I asked if she would mind if I took a bath. Since I had started working at age thirteen, I had a need to break the work day from my own time by taking a bath. The hot water marked the border between my world and theirs. Tonight there was another reason as well. I knew we were going to make love and I wanted to be clean for her. Since my tub was in the kitchen and there were no doors between the rooms, it meant she could watch as I bathed. She did not. When I finished, I put on a robe and went to sit next to her. Joan Baez played on the phonograph, and we spoke half in English, half in Spanish about our lives. She asked me about my job, school; I asked her about her girlfriend, driving the taxi.

The room was dark. We always met in darkness it seemed. I knew that soon she would touch me and I was already wet with wanting her. Here, now, on the bed all the offerings would be tested. We both had power in our hands. She could turn from me and leave me with my wetness, my need – a vulnerability and a burden. I could close up, turn away from her caring and her expertise. But neither happened. With extreme tenderness she laid me down. We kissed for a few minutes, and soon her hands knew I was not afraid. She smiled above me. 'I know why you took that bath, to be clean for me.' We began caring but demanding love-making. As I rose to her, she said, '*Dámelo, Juanita, dámelo.*' I strained to take and give to her, to pour my wetness in gratitude upon her hands and lips. But another part of me was not moving. I was trying so hard to be good for her, to respond equally to her fullness of giving, that I could not come.

She reached for pillows and put them under my hips. My legs opened wider. I held Esther's head in my hands as her tongue and fingers took my wetness and my need. I had never felt so beautiful. She reached deep into me, past the place of coming, into the center of my womanness. But I could do no more. I put my hand over her lips and drew her up along my body.

'Please, no more. It feels wonderful, and you have given me deep, deep pleasure.'

'Come home with me, I have things that will help.'

I knew she meant a dildo, and I wanted her to know it was not a lack of skill or excitement that was stopping me. It was her forty years of wisdom, her seriousness, her commitment to herself, and now her promising of it to me, that scared me. She lay still beside me; only her slenderness made lying on that small bed possible. I turned to touch her, but she took my hand away from her breast. 'Be a good girl,' she said. I knew I would have to work many months before Esther would allow me to find her wetness as she had found mine. The words, the language of my people, floated through my head – *untouchable, stone butch*. Yet it was Esther who lay beside me, a woman who trembled when she held me. Before she left she told me if I ever needed to reach her in the afternoons, she was next door sitting with an old woman, *una vieja*, a woman she had known for years who was now alone. She gave me the woman's number.

The next day was Saturday, and I spent the morning worrying about what I had done, my failure to perform. One-night stands are not simple events: sometimes in that risk-taking a world is born. I was washing my hair in the sink when I heard a knock at the door. Expecting a friend, I draped the towel around my naked shoulders and opened the door to an astonished delivery man. He thrust a long white box toward me as he turned his head. I took the box and closed the door. I had never had a messenger bring me a gift before. Twelve red roses lay elegantly wrapped in white tissue paper, a small square card snuggled between the stems:

Gracia, por todo anoche,
De quien te puede amor profundamente
Y con sinceridad – Esther

For one moment the lower East Side was transformed for me: unheard of elegance, a touch of silk had entered my life. Esther's final gift. We never shared another night together. Sometimes I would be walking to work and would hear the beeping of a horn. There would be Esther rounding the corner in her cab with her passenger who thought she was a man.

Lesbian Memories 1: Riis Park, 1960

I may never change my name to nouns or sea or land or air, but I have loved this earth in all the ways she let me get close to her. Even the earth beneath the city streets sang to my legs as I strode around this city, watching the sun glint off windows, looking up at the West Side sky immense as it reached from the river to the hills of Central Park. Not a Kansas sky paralleled by a flat earth, but a sky forcing its blue between the water towers and the ornate peaks that try to catch it.

And then my deepest joy, when the hot weekends came, sometimes as early as May but surely by June. I would leave East Ninth street early on Saturday morning, wearing my bathing suit under my shorts, and head for the BMT, the start of a two-hour subway and bus trip that would take me to Riis Park – my Riviera, my Fire Island, my gay beach – where I could spread my blanket and watch strong butches challenge each other by weightlifting garbage cans, where I could see tattoos bulge with womanly effort and hear the shouts of the softball game come floating over the fence.

The subway wound its way through lower Manhattan, out to Brooklyn, and finally reached its last stop, Flatbush Avenue. I always had a book to read but would periodically cruise the car, becoming adept at picking out the gay passengers, the ones with longing faces turned toward the sun waiting for them at the end of the line. Sometimes I would find my Lesbian couple, older women, wide-hipped, shoulders touching, sitting with their cooler filled with beer and cold chicken.

The last stop was a one-way, long station, but I could already smell the sea air. We crushed through the turnstiles, up onto Flatbush Avenue, which stretched like a royal highway to the temple of the sea. We would wait on line for the bus to pull in, a very gay line, and then as we moved down Flatbush, teenagers loud with their own lust poured into the bus. There were hostile encounters, the usual stares at the freaks, whispered taunts of *faggot, lezzie, is that a man or a woman*, but we did not care. We were heading to the sun, to our piece of the beach where we could kiss and hug and enjoy looking at each other.

The bus rolled down Flatbush, past low two-story family houses, neighborhoods with their beauty parlors and pizza joints. These were the only times that I, born in the Bronx, loved Brooklyn. I knew that at the end of that residential hegemony was the ocean I loved to dive into, that I watched turn purple in the late afternoon sun, that made me feel clean and young and strong, ready for a night of loving, my skin living with salt, clean enough for my lover's tongue, my body reaching to give to my lover's hands the fullness I had been given by the sea.

I would sit on the edge of my blanket, watching every touch, every flirtatious move around me, noting every curve of flesh, every erection, every nipple hard with irritation or desire. I drank in the spectacle of Lesbian and gay men's sensuality, always looking for the tall dark butch who would walk over and stand above me, her shadow breaking the sun, asking my name.

And the times I came with my lover, the wonder of kissing on the hot blanket in the sunlight, the joy of laying my head in her lap as we sat and watched the waves grow small in the dusk. The wonderful joy of my lover's body stretched over me, rolling me into the sand, our wrestling, our laughter, chases leading into the cooling water. I would wrap my legs around her, and she would bounce me on the sea, or I would duck below the surface and suck her nipples, pulling them into the ocean.

Whenever I turned away from the ocean to face the low
cement wall that ran along the back of our beach, I was forced
to remember that we were always watched: by teenagers on
bikes, pointing and laughing, and by more serious starers who
used telescopes to focus in on us. But we were undaunted. Even
the cops deciding to clean up the beach by arresting men
whose suits were judged too minimal, hauling them over the
sand into paddy wagons, did not destroy our sun.

Only once do I remember the potential power of our people
becoming a visible thing, like a mighty arm threatening
revenge if respect was not paid. A young man was brought
ashore by the exhausted lifeguards and his lover fell to his
knees, keening for his loss. A terrible quiet fell on our beach,
and like the moon drawing the tides, we formed an ever-
growing circle around the lovers, opening a path only wide
enough for the police carrying the stretcher, our silence threatening our anger if this grief was not respected. The police,
sinking into the sand under the heavy weight of their uniforms,
looked around and stopped joking. Silently they placed the
dead youth on the stretcher and started the long walk away
from the ocean. His lover, supported by friends, followed
behind, and then like a thick human rope, we all marched after
them, our near-naked bodies shining with palm oil and sweat,
men and women walking in a bursting silence behind the body,
escorting it to the ambulance, past the staring interlopers. The
freaks had turned into a people to whom respect must be paid.

Later in my life I learned the glories of Fire Island, the
luxury of Cherry Grove. But this tired beach, filled with the
children of the boroughs, was my first free place where I could
face the ocean that claimed me as its daughter and kiss in
blazing sunlight the salt-tinged lips of the woman I loved.

This Huge Light Of Yours

For Arisa Reed, for whom I did not keep
the porch light burning bright enough

The sixties is a favorite target of those who take
delight in the failure of dreams. For those who dabbled in social
change or who stayed aloof from the passion of the times, the
sixties has become a playground for nostalgia, a pot-filled room
of counter-culture adolescents playing with anger. But it is a
sad cynicism that jeers at the defeat of courage and commitment, and a selfish one too.

There is one group of Americans that cannot play with the
sixties, cannot give those years back to mockery and disdain. In
Alabama and Mississippi and Arkansas, in Watts and Harlem
and Philadelphia, in luncheonettes and in movie theaters, on
beaches, on school steps, and on buses, Black Americans took
history into their own work-worn hands, carried it on their
tired feet, until it became a different thing.

> Monday, March 15, 1965 was a notable day . . . In Alabama
> early that morning, Wilcox County's first black voter of the
> twentieth century was registered.*

This was after Jimmie Lee Jackson was murdered, after Rev.
Reebes was killed, after hundreds were clubbed and beaten
in Selma and Montgomery, after thousands were jailed, after
endless months of children walking in hate-filled streets, after
mothers and fathers and sons and daughters stood against

* *Protest At Selma* by David Garrow (Yale University Press, New Haven, 1978).

guns, tear gas, horses, whips, water hoses, against city police, state police, and the national guard. A country that does not know how to honor this heritage becomes a nightmare to its own people and to the world, becomes Reagan's America.

Selma, Alabama
1422 Washington Street
April 9, 1965

Hi Joan,

It was a great pleasure to receive a sweet letter from you and Ramona was so thrilled to have a letter of her own.

Monday I went to the Court house to get registered, but I didn't get in before closing time so I'll try again on the 19th.

Judy doesn't live with us now. She has a room in the project near the Church, but we keep in touch with each other and we all miss both of you very much. It was a pleasure to have had you live with us.

Things here now are not as strong as they were when you were here, but they are going to pick up in a day or so. We still have mass meetings and sing all those Freedom Songs.

I didn't have any stationery paper, but I wasn't going to let that stop me from writing.

Everybody here is doing just fine. We are still praying the same prayer and that one day We Shall Overcome.

We will be glad to have you at any time. I'll start burning the porch light on the last day of May looking for you.

We Shall Overcome,
Mrs M. Washington
Lower East Side, 1965

Carol had left me. I found a small one-room apartment on East Sixth Street between Avenues A and B. Here in this compressed tenement, guarded day and night by a huge Polish man who sat framed in the always-open door of his ground floor apartment in a chair that seemed to disappear under him, with his gout-stricken legs stretched in front of him, I took refuge. I joined the others who were also much reduced in circumstances.

Black and white, young and old, children and adults, we crammed the sorrows and angers of our lives into the hard squareness of those small rooms.

My fire escape was both a gift to me and to the neighborhood junkies. It provided me with another room in the hot evenings, and it gave them a freeway into my apartment. Clocks, radios, television, phonograph all disappeared with a regularity that became less frightening each time. Once I came home and saw the record albums strewn on the floor. A careful selection had been made; I felt I was in the middle of a conversation with people I had never met.

I would not give up access to the open air, however, and one afternoon, my faith was proved right. I was sitting at my table in front of the open window, typing a paper for school. I looked up to think for a moment and saw a tiny grey head poking into the room. It was Catly, as I came to call her. She looked around, looked at me and the small room, then turned and disappeared. I went back to work, but stopped in amazement a short time later. The small grey cat had returned, only this time she had a smaller cat dangling from her mouth, the first of six kittens she would bring through the open window and deposit on the floor of my room. Catly never gave up her wandering ways, and I became the foster mother of her squirming brood. The Lower East Side, with its shabbiness and wonders, its freedoms and reductions, its tough little joys and unexpected havens, was much like my open window.

Because my television had disappeared in one of the early forays of my unknown visitors, I had not seen the images of hatred that were pouring out of Alabama that March: the Black men, women, and children beaten with the flailing clubs of Jim Clark's men; the hoses turned full force on the peaceful marchers, washing away the grip of held hands, pushing, slamming people against the earth, the trees, each other, the dogs teeth bared in never ending snarls – all these forces marshaled against a band of would-be voters.

But I had ridden freedom buses into Philadelphia and Baltimore, had hidden from thrown rocks, had washed spit

from my face and hair, had sat with CORE* comrades at soda
fountains while the no-trespassing laws were read to us, and
had been dragged out of restaurants that Black CORE members
could not even enter. We, the white protesters, acted as a fifth
column. Usually under the leadership of a minister, we would
enter one of the segregated restaurants, pretending to be quiet
couples. Then we would join each other at a table, remembering never to eat or drink anything that was on the table, not
even the water. At a given signal we would all rise, and the
respectable air of the restaurant would be broken by the
minister reading a statement announcing who we were and
that we would not leave until our Black comrades, who were
now picketing and shouting outside the restaurant, were
allowed to join us. This simple act of opening the door to all
Americans never happened during these early years. Instead,
the police were called, we were read our warnings, and
then dragged out to join the demonstration. As whites, we were
useful for infiltration, but what we learned was the unforget-
table curse of our privilege.

I wore a double mask in these early sixties years, in those
white restaurants. My first deception was to the enemy: the
pose of a nice white person who could be let in and would
sit down and eat in quiet tones, ignoring the battle for human
dignity that was happening outside the windows. The second
was to my friends: the pose of straightness, the invisibility of my
queerness. They did not know that when the police entered,
with their sneers and itchy fingers, I was meeting old antagon-
ists. Perhaps their uniforms were a different color, but in the
Lesbian bars of my other world I had met these forces of the
state. I never told my comrades that I was different because a
secret seemed a little thing in such a time of history.

Although I did not have the images flickering across a black
and white screen, I had seen the photographs in the papers, the
large Black woman held to the ground by three white sheriffs,
a nightstick across her throat, her skirt pushed up above her
knees. All of us had seen and heard what was happening

* Congress of Racial Equality

in Selma. There was no place to hide. The night of the first attempt to cross the Edmund Pettis Bridge – the night of the brutal attack on a citizens' army – Judith, a straight friend, called to tell me what she had seen on television, and to ask me if I would go with her to Selma, Alabama to do voter registration work.

I looked around me, at the loss of love my life had become, at the hate that threatened all love, and I wanted to go, to do battle with another enemy besides my own despair, to use my body not for love-making but for filling the ranks in the struggle to change history.

The next day Judith and I joined the small exodus that was taking place all over America. We both had never traveled to the deep South before. We first flew to Atlanta to make connections for the flight to Selma. Once in the airport, our backpacks and Northern white faces loudly proclaimed us as the new breed of hated carpetbaggers. The Atlanta airport was like a troop station during the war, except that both sides were visible and in close contact with each other. Scattered throughout the terminal were groups of young people with their sleeping bags, nuns and priests in larger groups talking quietly, small suitcases resting against their legs.

We milled around, drawing closer to each other as the anger around us grew more distinct. Trapped into serving people they despised, the ticket agents could only load their responses with veiled verbal threats. As the young man handed us our ticket to Selma, he slowly looked us over and said, 'Going to Selma, huh. Well, we'll make sure you have a reeeel goooood tiiiime,' the words dragged out with controlled rage. This small taste of belligerence in the face of threatened change was the beginning of my understanding of what Black Southern Americans had been enduring and of the courage of the civil rights workers who had been living with threats against their lives every day. Like the other travelers bound for Selma, we discovered that we had to spend the night in the airport, and so we attached ourselves to a group of nuns, sticking closely to them like the long-necked birds that walk in the shadow of elephants. The one place that seemed safe to sleep in was the women's bathroom, and for the next six hours we huddled on the tile floor waiting for the morning light.

Early the next day our flight was announced, a small propeller plane that bounced its way to Selma. Nauseated by the mixture of fear and motion, I vomited during the flight, holding the white bag over my face as the reddish flats of the Selma countryside angled up toward us. Once on the ground, we were greeted by Jim Bevel, his head covered by an embroidered skull cap, his clear direct eyes looking straight at us, the small group of Northern do-gooders. He said, 'I hope you will be there when we come to New York.' We knew immediately we were no more than what we are, still part of the killing problem, and he treated us as if we were tourists who had signed up for some offbeat adventure vacation. His gait and the lines around his eyes told us that for him this was a war he could not walk away from: he would make do with whatever troops he had.

We were taken to a small caravan of cars and driven to the African Methodist Episcopal Church, which would become known to us as Brown's Chapel, to be welcomed and gathered up by the Black families who would house us and show us the ways of surviving white hatred while we were there. The church was packed with families and civil rights workers, many fanning themselves as they looked over the new arrivals. Judith and I were called up to the stage and introduced to the congregation. The minister asked who would like to give us a place to stay, and Mr and Mrs Washington raised their hands. So did Ramona, their eight-year-old daughter. We went to meet them and were introduced to their older son, Walt, who quietly and courageously was to save our lives several weeks later. We went to their house, a white house with a wraparound porch and trees in the front yard on a block of similar houses, not far from the church, but beyond the housing project where many of the other workers would be staying.

We entered their home quietly, feeling the wonder of what had happened in this small Southern town. Mrs Washington brought us to their main bedroom at the front of the house and told Judith and me that that was where we would sleep. We said no, that we had sleeping bags and that the floor or a couch was fine. Mrs Washington insisted. We must sleep in their big comfortable bed while we are guests in their home. We picked you, she added, because you look clean. Her kindness and the domestic serenity of the bedroom again reminded me of the secret I carried, my queerness, and I feared I would not have been taken into this home if my Lesbian self had stood in the church with me. But I accepted the weight of my disguise because I was so honored to be in this home and so moved to be even an infinitesimal part of this history. The room was peaceful, filled with the life of a long marriage. White ruffled curtains framed the small windows, photographs sat on the worn dresser, and the bed creaked comfortably with layers of shared sleep. The whole moment, as I sat on my side of the bed with Judith changing for the night, was filled with the awe of what events can do, with an awe for the graciousness and beauty of the human spirit, of the Washingtons, who in the midst of this terrible battle turned over their comfort and their most intimate place to two white Jewish women from New York whom they had never seen before. It was as if hatred had caused the usual flow of events to unravel and reveal another world of possibilities below.

The night was not peaceful. Judith, while knowing I was a Lesbian, had never slept in the same bed with me before. Every time our bodies accidentally touched, she leaped to the other side of the bed. But the coming events were to make this discomfort with each other insignificant. Our assignments for the next two weeks separated us, and Judith never slept with me in the Washingtons' home again.

All our days started at Brown's Chapel, and it was there that we learned where we would be needed for the week's activities. I was assigned to a group doing voter registration work in the poor, flat farmlands surrounding Selma. We moved around the countryside in a car covered with red dust, a cadre of workers led by Bill, an older SNCC* worker who was well

* Student Nonviolent Coordinating Committee

known to the families we visited. We were two white male ministers, and Ajax, a Black divinity student who was to become a special friend, and myself, the only woman. On our first ride out, I watched the male interaction closely, realizing I had to learn the language of this new world.

In the beginning I felt like a foreigner in many ways: to the religious discussions, to the land we were moving through, in the homes of the tenant farmers who stopped their work to listen to us, in the small, bare Baptist churches we visited to encourage community organizing and to give hope to the isolated groups that had already formed and were facing the anger of the whites around them. But we had work to do, and eventually my differences just became part of the pack I carried. I soon learned that while Bloody Sunday had shocked some of us into involvement, the struggle to gain voting rights had been going on in these counties for almost a year. The men, women, and children who had responded to the call for action by the SNCC and SCLC* workers were now a family of peaceful resisters who were wise in their knowledge of the forces arrayed against them and who knew they would not be turned around. However isolated, however small the gathering, the sense of unity was dazzling.

One day our car pulled into a dirt road in front of a wood church and inside waiting for us was a group of Black young men and women standing in a circle to greet us. We joined the circle, the March sun streaming in through the high windows and making patches of light on the bare wood floor. Around the circle we went saying our names, and for the visitors, why we were there and where we had come from. When it came to Ajax, he told his real name and then added his nickname, saying 'I heard you had some dirt down here, and I came to help clean it up.' The congregation of grassroots activists laughed, and everything seemed possible.

Later in the day as we were driving away from a visit to a tenant farmer's home on a dirt road that lined a newly tilled field, a trooper's car appeared behind us, coming out of the dust we had

* Southern Christian Leadership Conference

stirred up along the road. Our driver, Bill, turned his head and told us to be careful and quiet. All around us stretched loneliness, featureless earth in never-ending barren squares. We came to a stop, and the trooper pulled in behind us. I turned my head, peering out the dust-covered back window and saw a figure walking toward us who looked like a caricature of all I had heard about Southern sheriffs, except this was a real person. The sun glinted off the silver discs of his glasses, his hand rested on top of his gun which he wore low over his wide stomach. He was big and square, and his face was tight with anger.

Reaching the side of our car, he bent over and said to Bill, 'Get out of that car, boy.' The SNCC worker was a grey-haired man, lean and tall. Bill moved out of the car, almost as if he was bored. The trooper made him stand spread-eagle with his hands flat on the roof of the car as he frisked him, lecturing Bill about getting his passengers out of the county if he knew what was good for him and stopping stirring up trouble. We, the white Northern visitors to this landscape, sat in a silence that choked us, knowing we could go back home, back to a world where troopers didn't appear from nowhere and put a gun to your head. But this man, our teacher and protector, would not leave; his life and his family's life would be shadowed by this hunk of hatred. Bill slowly pulled his long body back into our little car and said it was time to call it a day. We returned in silence to the haven of Brown's Chapel.

That afternoon was the first time I learned that fear had a taste, that terror could make you clench your ass muscles to keep from soiling yourself. All in one day – the circle of sunlight and hope and courage, and the dryness of brutality.

The days and nights settled into a known routine. I would rise early and help prepare Mr Washington's breakfast, learning to make his coffee the way he liked it. He was a big, gentle man, always dressed in the blue dungaree overalls that he wore for work and that the male civil rights' workers wore for uniforms. We would sit together in the large kitchen at the back of the house with Ramona running around getting ready for school and for her time at Brown's Chapel. All my fantasies about what a father would be like found a home in Mr Washington, and his protective kindness became the symbol of the world I had discovered in Black Selma. Not that he couldn't get angry. He was – at the beatings, at the dangers his children faced, at the way his wife was treated by the white women she worked for, at how their livelihood was endangered because he believed in his people's right to vote – but to me he was a tree of kindness.

The mornings would be spent in front of Brown's Chapel, greeting the hundreds that were arriving every day: the nuns, young and strong-looking, the blond clean-cut ministers, the scruffy hippies, and the students from all over, Jewish and Christian, Black and white. The SNCC and SCLC workers moved among us, organizing the new arrivals, caucusing in small groups, mapping the goals and dangers of each day. For several days there were marches into downtown Selma. During one of them, Ajax was clubbed in the head as he bent his body over a fallen woman. I saw him the next day with his head swathed in bandages, the ever-present paperback on a philosophical theme protruding from his back pocket. His spirit was not daunted, but a seriousness seemed to anchor his short solid body closer to the ground.

We all gathered back at the church as soon as it got dark, hundreds of us pouring in there through the double wooden doors, coming home after the tensions of the day. As the night sky grew darker, the troopers would gather their cars around the chapel, turning their bright lights on its white wood walls, sitting or standing by their cars with their rifles cradled in their arms. Sometimes we would hear the voice of Bull Moose Clark come booming out over his loudspeaker. Every night hundreds of workers and families packed into the church built for fifty or sixty people, knowing the enemy had an easy target if his rage spilled over and he refused to respect the sanctuary of the church. This was America in 1965, and as we stood in our rows singing 'This Little Light of Mine', we knew a mighty battle was raging and would rage long after the church's lights had been shut off for the night. It would rage on into the years, and above the shouted ugliness of the bullhorns would soar the sweet shining voices of the youngsters who always sat in front of the chapel, right under the altar, their heads rocking from side to side, their hands raised in big claps swinging from side to side, giving the rest of us the beat of hope.

Some nights after we left the church but had too much nervous energy to go to bed, we gathered in a large one-room grocery store and restaurant that served as a social center for the Black community. We filled the room, a tired crowd of dusty and rumpled workers, downing beers and Cokes while we listened to whoever felt the need to speak out about the day's events. Here in this room was one version of the living flesh of the sixties. We were a mass of differences. Even our voices spoke in the accents of different geographies – the sharp New England twang, the harsher, fuller vowels of the Bronx and Brooklyn, the soft drawls of the South and the West – but here we put aside the places we had come from and listened to the place we were in. Here we heard the stories about daily life in Selma if you were Black and involved in the civil rights struggle.

In quiet voices we were told about the friends who disappeared off the streets and were never seen again, about the bodies found floating in back country rivers, about the beatings. We sat with our arms around each other, laid our heads on shoulders, just rested and felt safe for the few hours we were there. In the face of this history, and in that large worn room, we shared a tenderness perhaps only warriors without weapons know.

I sat at one of the few tables across from a short, curly-haired young man from New York one evening, who was questioning the meaning of the world in that special way New Yorkers have. He was filled with personal doubt and sounded as if he were sitting in a Greenwich Village cafe throwing existential challenges to the world. Next to me sat a young minister, his arm draped across my shoulders. Ajax stood leaning on the counter, and all the others, in their overalls and tired faces, were listening gently to the New Yorker's self-involved monologue. We all knew that he was a new arrival, holding on to what he had come with and not yet seeing what Selma would ask of him. The minister waited till he finished, then reached out and smoothed the young man's lowered head. 'We have come here with secrets,' he said. His words raced inside of me and I wanted to shout mine, but one neurotic New Yorker was not enough for any movement that night, I laughingly said to myself.

The contrast between the safety of that room and the world outside became terribly clear one night. Judith and I had over-stayed our time. We had all been warned to be off the streets by nine o'clock, but lulled by the camaraderie we felt, we stayed until after ten. We put on a brave face and refused escorts home, stepping into the night air and walking quickly until we came to the highway we had to cross. All of a sudden a pick-up truck filled with men, their faces shining like white moons, roared toward us. We saw the rifles cradled in their arms, and their voices came loud and clear: 'We're going to get you, you nigger lovers.' Judith and I started to run across the highway, down the long sidewalk, pushing at the limbs of the full trees to clear our way. In our panic, we soon became aware that someone was running after us and we looked desperately for the porch light that Mrs Washington always kept shining for us. With a final burst of speed, we made it to the safety of the light. Out of the night we soon saw who our pursuer was. Walter, the Washington's oldest son, had waited for us outside the store to make sure we made it home all right. Judith and I collapsed into nervous giggles, like schoolgirls afraid of being caught in some slight offense, but the sight of Walter, standing there, thin and shy, quickly silenced us. This was no game, no prank; this was a time and place where Black children died because they wanted to be free.

While we spent the week doing voter registration work, plans were proceeding for another march over the Edmund Pettis bridge. One night in the church, white index cards were given out to the visitors who wanted to be part of the new assault on Highway 80. We were asked to identify ourselves, list our organizational affiliations, our religion, our place of birth, and to write a short statement about why we wanted to go. We knew only a small number of the hundreds who had poured into Selma would be selected, and we sat in concentrated silence writing our best historical selves while the families fanned themselves and chatted. How ironic it must have seemed to them, to watch us vying for the honor of what they had done out of desperation and anger. Of course, we now had media protection. The wounds of three weeks earlier had been inflicted on plain folks; now the ranks of would-be marchers were swollen with politicians, newspeople, celebrities, clerics of many denominations, and Northern students like myself. Even the federal government was promising protection, and the eyes of this nation would be on those fifty-four miles.

I did not put the word *Lesbian* on my card. I put Jewish and feminist. I wrote about SANE and CORE. I did not talk about the bars I went to and the knowledge about bigotry I had gained from being a queer. I had no expectations of being selected, but the next night when the names were read, mine was among them. I was honored beyond belief. My friends kissed me, neighbors hugged me, Ramona jumped with delight and led me to the row of doctors and nurses who would accompany us. The final test was a brief physical exam to make sure the chosen ones were healthy enough for the walk. I stood next to a thin, freckled-faced nun who rolled up her habit's sleeve to have her blood pressure taken. We grinned at each other. Three hundred of us would eventually make the whole trip, and we would be led by those who risked their lives earlier in the month. The fear would come later, but that night and the next morning was filled with celebration and preparation.

The morning of the march, the Washingtons and I had a big breakfast together. Prayers were said asking for the safety of the marchers, and Mr Washington announced that he and Ramona would march with me for a little ways. We made plans to reunite the night before the final march into Montgomery, the night of the mass rally on the grounds of the St Jude Convent.

The sun shone brightly as 3200 people set out from Brown's

Chapel and followed the same route that had turned bloody three weeks before. We walked down Selma's main street, the jeering whites almost blocked from our vision by the phalanx of police that walked and rode alongside of us. As we crossed over the small bridge, the leaders stopped the march to commemorate the courage of those who had come before. You beat up on a hundred and a thousand return, one of them said. What I remember most of those early hours was the feel of my hand in Mr Washington's, the sight of his big farmer's body, and Ramona, chanting and singing on his other side. He and Ramona left me soon after we reached Highway 80, and then I settled into the rhythm of the walk. Singing, always singing, the red clay banks on one side of us and across the highway, the newly tilled cotton fields. We walked only seven miles that first day before we put up the big tents that would prove to be flimsy protection against the cold. The first night we all slept together, men and women, in whatever space we found. I shared a piece of cardboard with a Black minister from New Jersey. Cardboard became a much sought-after commodity, the only covering for the ground we had. The trucks with our sleeping bags had gone ahead, and because of a confusion, we would not see them again until the march was over.

The next day we did better. Our ranks were now pared down to the three hundred marchers who would go the whole way. We had a walking rhythm and covered sixteen miles that Monday. For some of us the walk was easy; we were young and strong. But there were others who struggled with the miles. That night, we were told we had to sleep in sex-segregated tents because the newspapers were claiming that sex orgies were going on in the night. We laughed at the rumors, but now I find it particularly interesting that sex and race were so immediately highlighted. My Lesbian self wondered at the futility of the precautions, and I became even more careful about my actions.

The March winds turned cold after dark, a bitter cold that few of us were prepared for. I spent long hours standing around the improvised heaters, large metal garbage cans filled with wood that we fed throughout the night. Like hobos, we surrounded the crackling fires, Black and white men and women trying to find some warmth in that Southern night. Tiredness eventually overcame me, and I walked into the huge women's tent, feeling lonely and careful. As I moved down the center aisle, I heard a voice call out, 'Joan, Joan over here.' It was one of the young women I had met in a church visit. She was lying on pieces of cardboard with three of her friends. A thin blanket covered them, and she offered to share it with me. I lay down with them. We huddled close together, trying to squeeze out what warmth we could.

On Tuesday the weather turned against us, but we had reached our destination, the large grounds of St Jude. We spent the day erecting tents and building the stage out of wooden caskets turned upside down. I remember especially a small hunchbacked white man who spent the day crawling over the coffins, hammering hour after hour. I helped prepare drinks for the workers and the incoming demonstrators. We set up huge kettles of lemonade in the middle of the field and ladled out hundreds of cups. Then Frank, a middle-aged Black man, and myself, walked the boundaries of the convent, serving the security guards. We talked about our lives as we made the rounds. He told me about his wife and how he wanted to leave the South. I told him about the Lower East Side but not about my women lovers. Again I felt the contradiction between kept silences and new honesties.

When we had filled the thirst of the workers, we found the Convent's kitchen. The huge kettles had to be washed out, and we needed running water. The kitchen was in the back of the building, and sitting in the open doorway were six older Black women wearing starched white uniforms and small white caps – the domestic staff for the Convent. All the nuns we had met were white. We asked permission to use the sink, and quietly they nodded their heads, staring at Frank and me the whole time. They had never seen a white woman do this work, Frank said, as we practically climbed into the pots.

Later that day as I was helping Ajax pull on one of the heavy tent lines, I heard my name called out. It was Judith, running across the field. We hugged, laughed, and promised to find each other when the march was over. She was to stay many more months than I.

I spent the rest of the day working with Ajax, and then we were given shelter in the convent. The nuns were particularly attentive to me when they discovered I was Jewish; one young woman gave me a pair of pajamas to change into and led me into a hidden cupboard so I could change without being seen. One of the male marchers was having tea in a small parlor right outside my improvised dressing room, and the nun was especially concerned that he did not see me. The pajamas had small hearts on them and were of a light seersucker fabric. I had not worn pajamas like these since I was a little girl. I was given the one available cot, while my comrades slept on the floor, on chairs pulled together, and on couches. I woke the next morning to a sweet-faced nun bending over me, her cross swaying before my eyes. For one minute I did not know where I was, and then I saw our muddy boots and I remembered.

That night, thousands poured into the campgrounds. I rejoined Judith and Ramona, and we stayed busy trying to keep an eye on her and get some sleep for the next day. Rain had turned the campground into a muddy swamp, but the big show with stars like Joan Baez and Shelley Winters still continued. We all sat in little wooden chairs sinking into the mud as the coffins became a stage. At some point, the huge lights went out. An argument broke out between the civil rights workers and the police, who refused to help. I was standing next to a mobile home, one of the many that housed the more famous marchers, when I saw a small group of workers, police, and national guardsmen approach the trailer. One of the workers pounded on the door, and a very drunk, very voluptuous Shelley Winters opened it. 'Help us, please Shelley,' the worker pleaded. 'We need the lights from the military trucks to light up the stage.' Winters was leaning out over the doorway of the van, her low-cut dress getting wet in the pouring rain. 'Honey, come here,' she said, in a slurred, amused voice, motioning to the national guard big shot. He approached, and she whispered something in his ear. He laughed and cupped his hand over her full breast. 'O.K., give them the lights,' he shouted to the gathered crowd.

When I got back to the tent, Judith had secured a sleeping spot for us, our number now grown by one. A tall, raw-boned, blonde woman had joined us. We slept that night, along with thousands of others, on a bed of warm mud. The morning light came slowly, and marchers stumbled out into the grey, glad the night was over and anxious for the final stage of the march to begin. Everywhere cries of recognition rang out, for people had kept arriving throughout the night, and old friends ran to greet each other. From under one of the tent flaps appeared Susan, my first woman lover. We just had time to shout hello to each other before we had to line up. Ajax joined me, and we waited for what seemed like hours for the thousands to assemble. At some point the sun came out, and then we moved, a huge rope of people, hands joined in long lines that stretched from one side of the road to the other. We turned a corner, and there was the capital building of Montgomery shining at the end of the broad street, a Confederate flag flying high above the national banner. Jeering white faces greeted us: the gesture I remember the most was man after man grabbing his crotch as the interracial lines marched by. Those last minutes seemed to fly, even though they were actual hours. Dr King spoke to us, helicopters flew overhead, ambulances and trucks filled with our gear roared up and down the streets. We had made it to the forbidden spot. What had started with blood and raw courage ended in a mass of 25,000 people besieging the Alabama state capital in the full glare of live television coverage.

But while the speeches went on, we were told over and over again by the SNCC and SCLC workers to get out of town fast. The fury that had lined the streets was beginning to spill over. As the sun went down, we lost the protection of the media, the illusion of a transforming victory. At eight o'clock that night, as marchers were being transported back to Selma, Viola Gregg Liuzzo, a volunteer driver, was shot to death by a carload of K.K.K. men on the same Highway 80 that we had sang and clapped our way down two days before. Ajax and I were among the thousands trucked to the airport only to discover that many of the major airlines were refusing to take us on. We finally found room on a charter flight belonging to a large group of Black Baptist ministers who were flying home to Philadelphia.

We were both numb with tiredness and emotional exhaustion, but we knew that he was coming home with me. I put out of my mind his words to me back in Montgomery when we were waiting to be picked up: 'The only group of people I can't stand are homosexuals.' We had been through so much together, and his goodness, his fine toughness, drew me to him. Once we reached Philadelphia we spent another night on the ground, this time the marble floor of the bus terminal, waiting for our connection back to New York. In the morning, we were treated like soldiers returning from a courageous or traitorous battle, depending on the politics of the spectator. Some people shouted obscenities at us; one Black taxi driver gave us two silver dollars to commemorate the Selma march. We were dirty, marked by that red clay. Our sleeping bags hung low on our backs. But when we finally emerged on to Forty-second Street, with the New York sun welcoming us home, all the grandeur of that time soared within us.

Ajax stayed with me for a week in my Lower East Side home. We made love, and he cried when he came in me. I held him tight to me and wondered at my own stillness. We talked of marriage, of opening an interracial orphanage. All of this was still the legacy of Selma. Then it was time for him to return home, to his studies at the divinity school. For another week we wrote to one another, and then I finally had to tell him I was a Lesbian, that I did not know what I could be in the future, but that he had to know that about me. I never heard from him again. I wrote two more begging letters, asking him just to talk to me, but I am sure Ajax felt a dream had been smashed.

But not the larger dream, Ajax, not the dream you had in that small, brave church somewhere in Lowndes County, Alabama. And I have carried Selma with me all these years as well, not to prove my Civil Rights credentials, for I know more than anyone how little I had really done in the face of lives that were committed every day, but because Selma is to me the wonder of history marked on a people's face and on their soul. Now all the secrets are out, and I can march against apartheid with the Lesbian Herstory Archives banner carried proudly in the open air, and all around me are other gay men and women joining voices with thousands more to say no to a killing racism and yes to a new world of liberated lives. I carry with me the belief that Mr and Mrs Washington would still greet me at their front door.

Selma, Alabama
Washington Street
April 9, 1965

Dear Joan,

Judy has moved to the projects so she can be closer to the Church. And I enjoyed reading your letter. And we enjoyed you and Judy staying with us. This mite be a short letter but I am glad mother reminded me to write you because I was getting ready for Easter program. I hope that you can come back and visit us again and I just mite have a surprise for you. Come back.

with love,
Ramona.

Lesbian Memories 2:
The Lower East Side, 1966

Rachel, Rachel
whore, whore
wore your hair down to the floor
and we laid our hearts at your silken door

We had all left something, all of us who careened down Second Avenue, pouring out of the side streets – East Sixth, East Ninth, East Twelfth – numbers and letters exact in their geographic depiction, their pureness of form covering the swelter of life that tumbled from apartment to apartment. Out we would pour on a hot June morning, running down the crumbling stairs of the old brownstones, leaving behind the three-room railroad flat with its tub in the kitchen and bathroom in the hall. Like much older and wiser exiles, we never opened our conversations with questions about our beginnings. Information about previous life just seemed to filter through or got filled in years later. We used our bodies, our actions, our costumes, the close proximity of our lives to tell our stories.

I don't know how I learned Rachel was a whore before I met her, but I did. Perhaps Meryl, who ran the head shop on Tenth Street, told me. Rachel of the Lower East Side and all points east. Flowing red hair down her back, like a slow-moving river, tall, thin Rachel who believed in the gospel of Tim O'Leary and earned her money turning tricks. Her one-room apartment was different from the ones I knew: hers had been redone into something called a studio. One square room filled with Rachel's bed, big enough for any position, covered with a zebra-print artificial fur and crowned with black satin pillows. Her kitchen was a countertop covered by the smallest appliances I had ever seen, an apartment kept up for her by her gangster boyfriend who was later found shot in the mouth, sprawled out in his car under a Lower East Side bridge – another piece of information that floated down and settled in my mind as the years went by. Just the same way I heard a year later that Rachel was now walking the streets of Indian cities looking for her guru, her red hair and tall slimness suspended in the hot morning air. Always by a river. For Rachel, all rivers were one: the East River floating its length into the Ganges, the Ganges reaching under the earth for the Amazon, the Amazon stretching its sinewy hand to the Nile, and the Nile starting slowly and then rushing to the Yangtze. Walking alongside of them all would be Rachel, bringing the water home in her body's touches. Rachel was a giver of dreams who lived in her own, dreams outlined in the hard need for money. For pleasure, she frequented our Lesbian bars, and when we were lucky, she took us home to roll in the length of her red hair.

One day, before our night of love-making, I saw her coming down the broad expanse of Second Avenue – the avenue that held all the wonders of the world, that sparkled like the Champs Elysée, which I had never seen, on its good days and which breathed sad histories on its bad ones. She was a languid yet forceful figure, ever-moving forward while parts of her trailed behind. She came closer and closer, laughter building up in her eyes. She wore, as always, a garment of her own creation, a white cotton sari that floated free behind her. The sun glinted off her colors, the red and white of her dreams. Rachel, the lewd queen of psychedelic hookers, and I, bound to the earth, a broad-hipped woman who couldn't hold a candle to this red-haired woman's loveliness, I watched her come to me as all the life of the wide street eddied around us. She stopped still in front of me, but her hair kept moving, and the air danced around her. She smiled, laughed, and pulled me to her, kissing me deeply, opening my lips for her tongue, entering and opening me right there in the street, with the Ratner regulars staring at us. Then, giving me a big wink, she picked up her stride once again and continued down the street.

This was the Lower East Side, a place where gifts were laid at your feet, given by those who seemed to have nothing, yet carrying in their eyes and on their hands a broken radiance.

Mara's Room

Darkness and light in the same place, both essential. More than twenty years ago, but in the memory a burning moment that singes surrounding time. Mara's kitchen table on Fourth Street: the round oak table stained with jam, crushed bananas, gritty with bread. The front room curtained with plants, books, papers cascading from hidden shelves. Mara's violin resting in a corner. I knew Mara's room best at night; a small oasis of light, powerful shadows on the walls. We would sit huddled over our books, the old texts of morality plays piping us into the dreams of the Christian past. The shepherds belched while the stars shone with divinity, and two Jewish women intent on the study of literature chanted the three Marys' breathless cry, 'Where has he gone?'

Mara is shining darkness within the light. Her lean body shaded by hip-length hair, her wide mouth, the unruly eyebrows, the dark restless caring eyes. She cavorts with ideas, running them like colts along the fence of her intelligence.

These were the Lower East Side days, New York University graduate school days – little money, bagels stolen from Ratner's that would last three days before turning into stone, days of study, of freedom, of physical roaming. Not the days of notoriety that would come later, but earlier, when the memory is of Slavic eggs and the smell of cabbage fermenting in the bathtub. The Russian Orthodox Church would chime its voice over Tompkins Park, reaching toward Second Avenue, and the treks to the toilets in the hall would begin. Every floor in my Ninth Street tenement would join the chorus of personal grunts as another day came to this old tolerant neighborhood.

Mara and I mostly lived our separate lives during the day. She was a married young mother whose husband was just beginning a career as an internist. Several nights of the week he slept at his job, leaving his young wife with all her restless energy caught at home between the crib and her desk. From time to time, Mara would break out of her dutifulness and become passionate over some young man, delighting in her sensuality in much the same way she enthused over the power of a new idea.

I lived alone in a three-room railroad flat on Ninth Street, putting my life back together after the loss of a woman I loved deeply. I grew strong on the familiar challenge of piecing together daily queer survival. My life was a mix of boring clerk jobs, brave friends, bar adventures, one-night stands, and late night journeyings in the Forty-second Street Library trying to educate myself out of graduate school. I had known Mara several years before when we were both English majors at Queens College. Once in the early sixties, when we were on our way to a peace demonstration in Washington, I had confessed to her that I was a Lesbian. 'I just hope it doesn't ruin your life,' she said.

Now, both a little older, we sat at the table. My old want of her was back. I had never dared to cross the line between our worlds; husband and child stood as sentinels on the border. It was growing late this night, an old boyfriend had stopped by, and I could see that Mara had hours of talk left in her. Her husband was away at the hospital, and she had suggested I sleep over. 'I'm going to bed,' I told the circle of light, Mara and the man, their heads bowing in toward the yellow glow.

The bedroom was at the end of the hall, with the big double mattress squeezed against the baby's crib. Hearing her gentle breathing, I remembered an afternoon when Mara, glorying in the loveliness of her naked daughter, lay her own body on top of her daughter's, balancing on her elbows to save the child from her weight, the two so amazed with each other. Now the room is dark. I put on a white cotton nightgown of Mara's and turned on my stomach, dozing with the voices from the kitchen falling into my growing sleep.

Then silence; Mara, her body light in the darkness, kneeling beside me. 'Turn over and let me in.' Stumbling in my sleep, I turned, dazed by the power and suddenness of her command. She hung over me, and I knew our bodies were touching, yet it seemed as if only her hands carried her body's force. She pushed at me hard, opening my thighs. 'Let me in.' I was frozen by the collision of our worlds. I spread my legs slowly, but her rush came too quick. Her fingers roared into me. She kissed me hard, harder than any woman's lips I had known, hard as her fingers. Her tongue and teeth took me, cracking my lip, and I knew my blood was coming. I looked up at her, the immobile eye of her storm. She threw her head back with each thrust calling out her pleasure. 'Come to me, come to me.'

Oh Mara, how I wanted to come to you – down all the years of passion kept hidden under the long gowns the good wives wrapped around their secret wetnesses. The overwhelming possibilities of woman touch and entry, of passion and power had come to you in a startling instant. But I could not. I was frozen because for me you were a real woman, not a place of secret explosions. My clitoris could not bear your burden of history; my hips could not move against your whirlwind. You came in dazzling waves of freedom, you came on shores never to be visited again, and I knew even before your body slid back into its full weight that I had lost you again.

When the revelation had passed, you lay beside me. Carrying my history on my lips, I bent my head between your legs to taste, to soothe, to speak to you in the language of my love, but it was too much. You pushed my head away. The secret glory had burst and the curtains again descended, long heavy drapes of custom and of fear. There could be no acknowledged touch outside the frenzy of deliverance. The next morning, a kiss was not allowed. We stood before a mirror, Mara braiding her long hair, opening her face to the morning light. I stood behind her, a shadow, touching the crack in my lip with my tongue. The earth for one brief instant had split open, letting loose the storm of years, but now in the light, only a thin red line on a woman's lip marked the place where the center had burst.

Stone Butch, Drag Butch, Baby Butch

1.

New words swirl around us
and still I see you in the street
loafers, chinos, shades.
You dare to look too long
and I return your gaze,
feel the pull of old worlds
and then like a femme
drop my eyes.
But behind my broken look
you live
and walk deeper into me
as the distance grows between us.

Shame is the first betrayer.

2.

The birth of Lesbian feminism. New York. The old firehouse on
Wooster Street. Wooden chairs pulled across the cobbled floor.
Pretty young women form a circle to form a group called the
Lesbian Liberation Committee. Two old-time Lesbians arrive,
grey-haired, short DAs. They stay on the outskirts. I go to the

bathroom on the floor below. Two of the young women stand in front of me. 'Why do they have to look like men? I hope they don't come back.' When I returned upstairs, the grey-haired women were gone. They never returned. Jean and Ginny told the world who we were and what we wanted. Books were written saying the bad old days were over. The national organizations started, the presses and newspapers began, and the grey-haired women receded further and further, as if they had blended into the walls.

Shame is the first betrayer.

3.

Stone butch, drag butch, baby butch
the litany of the unwanted.
I see your eyes smoking
behind the self-congratulations
of the vegetarians
the Goddess worshippers
the healers.
Your magic worked in other places
in church alcoves
in diner toilets
in moving cars
pants with sharp creases
shirts cuffed
hair slicked back
riding Brooklyn subways
at five in the morning
shades worn just right
for mystery, for protection.
Rigid, you walked the gauntlet of their sneers
Hey lezzie, hey queer
and even when it was the end of the line
you kept moving.

A strange witch,
my baby butch.

4.

Stone butch, drag butch, baby butch
leaned me back against the bathroom door
tuned for the intrusion, you sucked my breast.
Alert and wanting, we made love in a public place
because territory was limited.
You pushed my wetness out
only when cunning had won for us a place.
In a subway station toilet
I held your head between my thighs
heard the roar and thought it was
our secret rushing out.

5.

Stone butch, drag butch, baby butch
Sandy tells me of the time
she walked in Prospect Park
with her lover on her arm.
Forgetting they were freaks,
they let the bending trees
caress their day.
The men, outraged by Sandy's pants
and Carol's skirt,
attacked with chains.
The women fled,
past playgrounds
past the benches made for lovers.
Sandy, smiling, says
through all the years
they never hurt me,
but we both know better.

6.

A hot dark night on Eighth Street.
Held tight with love,
the butch yells up to a shadow on the wall
all she can see of her lady
who calls out
'I'm here baby'
and we all hear her.
A shrine for separated lovers,
the Women's House of D.*
They tore it down
replaced it with a garden
but those voices still are there
the lasting blossoms of our surviving time.

Stone butch, drag butch, baby butch
I keep you deep within me
warning voices in a changing time.
Shame is the first betrayer.

* The Women's House of Detention stood for many years on the corner of Eighth
Street and Sixth Avenue in Greenwich Village.

Two Women:
Regina Nestle, 1910–1978,
And Her Daughter, Joan

When my mother died, she left me two satchels of scribbled writings. Many of these fragments were written on the back of long yellow ledger sheets, the artifacts of a book-keeper. She had started writing in the last years of her life, sitting in apartments empty except for a bed, television set, table and chairs. Dressed in a housecoat, her work clothes put away for that day, she would sit on the edge of the bed, using the chair as her table. Scattered on one side of her would be the day's racing forms and OTB stubs; on the other side would be her writings. An overflowing ashtray shared the chair seat with her pad, and a few feet away, the television spoke to her, bringing the smooth voice of the public broadcasting system into the room. She would sit with her legs spread apart, her glasses low on her nose, a cigarette burning in one hand, and write messages to her daughter, her son, her lover at the time, or to the psychiatrist she had met at Bellevue when she was found wandering the city streets not quite remembering who she was.

Regina Nestle was born into a poor Jewish family in 1910 and raised in Manhattan. She left school at fourteen to work in the garment district as a bookkeeper, married Jonas Nestle in 1928, was widowed in 1939 and left with a five-year-old son, Elliot, and a daughter yet to be born. Our family of three was pared down by the psychological dictates of the late forties and early fifties. My brother, unhappy and confused by his father's death, screamed out his anger in frightening tantrums. Get him away from home, the doctors said, away from the family of women. From age fourteen, he fled our family; he entered the army at sixteen to make the final break. Through the years, I too wanted to flee this woman whose passions overflowed, making whatever security we had achieved so impermanent. Her sexual longings, her uncontrollable gambling, her continuous need for money to stave off the eviction notices, the loans come due, the liens on her salary, seemed to endanger my life. In 1959, I took refuge on the Lower East Side where apartments were cheap.

Over the years, I learned much more about Regina Nestle, about her strength, her ability to keep coming back, her laughter, and her courage. And then time collapsed. In 1978 she had a massive heart attack. She had been stricken just as I left for work. When she called a doctor, he told her to put herself in a cab, but she had no money, was unable to dress herself. So she waited those hours for me to come home. Again it was just the two of us, with the same mixture of desperation and absurdity. I dressed her. I couldn't get an ambulance to take her to the hospital her doctor wanted. I hailed a gypsy taxi driver and we sped through New York. My mother was shouting, 'Hurry up please hurry up oh God,' almost as if she were giving birth. And then I was standing by her bed in the hospital, stroking her cheek, telling her I loved her, taking her scribbled notes begging for release from the respirator. She turned her face into my hand, and I realized how small she was, how my hand reached from her forehead to her chin, how alone we were – no husband, father, son – only me, her daughter and, when she could, Deborah, my lover. Ten days later, my mother died. The last time we saw Regina, she was sitting on the edge of her hospital bed, head bent, reading Deborah and me the poem she had written to thank the nurses for bringing her back to life.

Why have I had to write about my mother's life, Regina's life? The rules she broke, the knowledge she had of her difference, the things she told me that mothers were not supposed to tell their daughters – as if she knew I needed this to survive in my life of sexual difference – all this is one reason. And I want to give her a final gift, one she wanted desperately, that her writing move beyond the bed and the chair. Finally, I want to take back something that was denied me by the medical and psychological world that told me Lesbianism was a sickness, that my feelings about my mother were distorted, infantile, mannish. So I ran, like my brother did, driven by the doctors' threats. Some will read this and say, 'No wonder she is a Lesbian.' This is the voice I have fought my whole life. It is for the others that I write in the hope that some part of this will make it easier for us to stop running.

My mother was a bookkeeper. She had kept the books of men ever since she was thrown out of the protective circle of married women by the death of her husband in her twenty-ninth year, 1939. I was born five months after my father's death, so I never knew my mother when she was not the keeper of someone's books. The week before she died, in her sixty-eighth year, she had gotten a part-time job keeping the books for two women weavers; she was sure this job would be different.

Joe's death was quick, painful, and not merciful. He wanted to live; he was young, vital, had a son he adored and wife that sufficed. He tried so hard to survive and when we parted at the hospital, knowing he could not make it, he asked me how I was going to manage. I told him to let go. I would make it but more importantly, his child and the child to come surely would. The last words between two who had created life.

Joan was born five months later, and in those five months, all values, all images of family, of compassion were destroyed. The desertion by the families brought to me the realization that all were frightened people. I got along, and the coin of life was money. I accepted their law and rejected them. I picked up the challenge. The people I had contact with were mostly my own tribe, Jews, and I saw them battling the world to make it.

In my early years, when we were still together, my mother would get up early every morning, put on a well-made dress and matching shoes, have several Chesterfields and cups of black coffee, and then disappear out of the door to go to the office. *The Office* was a magic word, one of the powerful nouns I grew up with. *Wholesale* was another, a word that meant having something. My mother's clothes were bought wholesale; she bemoaned the fact that I was too fat for the small sizes that hung on the showroom racks. Other creatures that I knew by name were *the line, the cutters, the showroom,* and always *the buyers.* I had images of huge scissors hanging from the ceiling, long wooden tables, and the hulking figure of the buyer stalking through endless rooms of floating dresses. My mother was part of the long tradition of women who toiled behind the showroom in windowless rooms, behind desks piled high with blue ledger books and overflowing metal mail cages. She lived with invoices, yellow perforated sheets spilling out all around her like uncontrollable tongues. In the office, my mother controlled in and out – the journeyings of endless pieces of paper that meant money for the boss and survival for her.

On the third finger of my mother's right hand was a bookkeeper's callous, a yellow raised hard cushion of skin formed by the pressure of her pen over the years as she listed figure after figure. The opposite of erosion, day after day, work had built up a plateau on my mother's hand.

The garment industry is run by illusionists, magicians, panderers to the world. The buyers are prostitutes. Give them what will please their customers, you own them. Displease their customers, you have lost security. Season after season, I was part of the cycle, saw the struggle, became part of it, dipped into the excitement of money, power, physical attraction, adornment, flattery, sensuality. Sex was like the afternoon cocktails, the theater tickets, the 'black market' bribery, the procuring of nylons – all trivialities but of paramount importance. You had something that someone else could not get. You had it made. It was easy and pathetic after paying off your first IRS man. How sometimes I wished they would set me free. You see, I didn't have

*the strength to do it myself. I was guilty and so was the world.
They had no values and neither did I, or so it seemed.*

*I saw less and less of my children. I had a housekeeper, effi-
cient. I was with the children on weekends. The total transition
from one world to another began to show its effects. It became
more difficult for me to live. Loneliness became my friend and
dreams became reality. The war, business, good food, clothes,
even the beauty of the children were dim.*

The Bronx, 1948: My mother, strong and beautiful, stands in
front of the foyer mirror, straightening the veil of a dark smart
hat, in a checkered dress, perfumed. I sit on the floor, looking
up at her, knowing already in my little girl's head that this is a
woman who is glorying in not being a mother and also knowing
that she is preparing for love-making. The housekeeper,
who keeps me clean and fed, sleeps with me while I lie awake
waiting for Regina to come home and take me to her bed, but
always the dawn comes before she does.

And then in a swirl of failure for reasons not explained to me
it all changed; the hat disappears, the housekeeper no longer
comes. Other caretakers keep me until my mother returns
from work. I sit in other children's homes, on their couches,
watch them eat dinner, see two parents, who, for a small fee,
will keep me until my mother comes to pick me up. The money
has disappeared, the job is a grinding everyday ordeal. We are
evicted from the Bronx apartment; a relative turns us away; we
have no place to live. My mother goes to the Hotel Dixie. I go to
my aunt Miriam and uncle Murray in Queens to sleep on their
grey couch in a grey room, grateful for the food and security,
believing that I have terribly betrayed my mother. I wished for
her alluring time to come again. Even at the end when she
walked Broadway in her bedroom slippers, I wanted to remind
her of the veil with its black stars, her upswept hair, arms firm
and strong fastening on her hat. I wanted the mother back who
was a woman who did not want to be a mother.

As soon as I was old enough, I went to the office with my mother on Saturdays. When I asked her why she had to work six days a week, she replied, 'The books have to get done.' The books ruled her life like religious texts; they prescribed her actions and contained the markings of her life. Before I was old enough to help her, she would give me pieces of paper to draw on, trying to keep me from my favorite toy, the metal racks with their iron wheels that I could ride across the waxed showroom floors. Poor men still push these racks through the garment district's congested streets, their arms bulging with the weight of each season's new line.

As I grew older, I would come to the office after school and sit watching Regina at work. How proud I was of this woman who could answer telephone calls, drink coffee, smoke a cigarette, turn the pages of her ledger sheets, and joke with her girls all at the same time. I was safe here and so was my mother, I thought then. No eviction notices, no one calling her a whore, no bill collectors shining their flashlights through the windows. It was Regina holding the world together. At some point she would take me around to meet everybody – the operators, the cutters, the shipping clerks and finally the boss. I knew it was very important that I be good on these tours, that I show the boss my mother could work a fifty-hour week and still raise a good kid. Through the years and the jobs, the tours of introduction continued but with some changes. I now knew my mother was sleeping with her bosses and they and the women my mother worked with knew I was a Lesbian. I no longer cared about being a good kid, but I did care about how shabby her office was, how she called the men who were fucking her Mister.

I lived with the garment industry the way other children lived with grandparents. At age eleven, I watched a call girl entertain a buyer and his drunken friends on an afternoon outing to a New Jersey beach. She sat, a beautiful young woman wearing a halter that fell low on her breasts, looking bored, waiting for one of the men to lurch up at her and take her into the tiny bungalow. I came closer to her and just watched. I wanted to break into her bored look, her placid tiredness, into the place that made her breasts swell. For one instant before she disappeared for another quick lay, she looked back at me. I understood she was a working woman, like my mother.

The firm names of the garment industry are cute: Young Togs, Mira Belle Fashions, Wendy Girl Dresses. They mask the desperate battle to survive each year. Every house has a genealogy in the market. My mother knew their lineage like the back of her hand. One of her jobs was to check credit ratings in Dun and Bradstreet. For a long time, I thought this was a street out of Dickens novel, a twisting, narrow road where quaint characters sat in front of their shops, shouting their worth. My mother worked fifteen years for a firm called Bon Dana, pulling her bosses through the 'black market' years, making the figures tell lies that earned thousands for her firm. Bon Dana sounded to me like the name of a small country with shady beaches, a country that demanded complete dedication from its citizens. Why and how my mother left Bon Dana I do not know, but it was the office that molded her, sharpened her manipulative skills, and let her know the range of greed she would have to find room for on her ledger sheets.

My mother, famous for her ability to pull the books together so the accountant had little to do on his yearly visit, laughed at the CPAs who made the big money while they marveled at her talent. The women were *bookkeepers*; the men were *accountants*. She taught me what a mixture of arrogance and failure her business world was, the class structure of its compact society, with the factory shop at one end (before they moved South), and the showroom at the other. The bookkeepers lived in the middle, not good enough to walk through the showroom but more powerful than the shopworkers because they did the payroll and controlled petty cash. In later years, my mother tried to be a workers' fifth column: she fought the bosses for raises for her girls and ran interference for the shopworkers who needed cash advances. It was a war fought by a woman against a man, the keeper of the books against the owner of the books. Like all those in bondage, my mother laughed at the master's dependency, at his vanities. She recorded his tax write-offs, his stealing from the business, his use of call girls to pleasure out-of-town buyers. While she was scorned as a social equal, she was feared as a woman who knew too much. My mother's whole life was marked by knowledge women were not supposed to have.

Did I love my husband? Such a definite question. Who was this husband? I had never considered the man who was the father of my children as my husband. I only knew the man. Did I love this man? Don't you see, Doctor, if I could answer you in one word yes I don't think I would have to be here. I remember as a little girl, the impatience with my own youth. I recognized that I was someone, someone to be reckoned with. I sensed the sexual order of life. I wanted to be quickly and passionately involved. I recognized my youth only in the physical sense as when I looked at my own body, saw the beautiful breasts, the flat stomach, the sturdy limbs, the piquant face, the eyes that hid sadness, needed love – a hell of a lot of grit, and already acknowledging this to be one hell of a life. I was going to find the key. I knew the hunger but I did not know how to appease it. I have not yet appeased it or reconciled myself. Therefore, Doctor, did I love my husband – yes but not as I wanted to, but I was a good wife, a passionate wife, a fearing wife.

My mother always said she had to be a man in a man's world but she wasn't. She was a different kind of woman, one for whom there was no vocabulary. She was a widow who, out of the necessity to support herself and her two children, developed a craftwoman's skill – the manipulation of endless figures. Her apprenticeship started in 1924, when she left school at fourteen to work in a furrier's office. The boss, Jonas Nestle, liked the smart young girl and married her. But my mother was already damaged goods. In that same fourteenth year, she had been raped by a group of men and a pregnancy had developed. She succeeded in finding a woman doctor who performed an abortion. My mother realized that Jonas would not marry her if he knew she was not a virgin. Desperate for her right to a safe life, she faked purity and managed to shed the right amount of blood. For a few years my mother kept no books. She was the glowing young wife and, in a few more years, the mother of a son, Elliot. She had girlfriends, Yetta and Rose the vegetarian, went to Coney Island with other young couples, smoked cigarettes on the roof of her Bronx apartment house so her husband would not yell at her. But then came the night of pain, and Jonas the strong young man died.

I started high school a ball of fire, with my twin sister. I believed we were God-sent. It was conveyed to us by the teachers, by our mother dressing us alike. All external. You know, Doctor, it was all bullshit. I never felt it. I was angry. I was unique. My twin sister, Miriam, had infantile paralysis at the age of three. Her lack of activity became my way of life. I sat, I knitted, I read. If I did anything physical that she could not I felt I was a selfish, ugly kid. Then I rebelled. At fourteen. I left school and went out into the business world. At fourteen I had my first sexual relationship.

Oh my mama, the things you liked to do
fuck and suck cock
one customer knocked your teeth out
but you would not let your woman friend in to help you
because he might come back and she would get hurt
so you lay in a pool of blood and teeth until the
police broke the door down.
You were evicted once again for being an undesirable
    tenant.
You went downhill fast. From quiet dinners with
your bosses who bedded you
in time to be home for *Shabbas*
to the merchant marine who doused himself with your
perfume while you knelt between his legs
and threatened to kill you every week if you didn't
turn over your paycheck

Oh mama the things I saw and the things you did.
No wonder you are a Lesbian they will say.
No the wonder is my mother
who taught me when to go on my knees
and when not,
who kept alive her right to sexuality when sex was killing
      her.

Jean was a misfit, but she didn't know it. At the age of fourteen, dark-eyed, short, a beautiful pair of breasts, a good behind, dimples, a Jewess, hot in the pants – that was the description. Almost perfect for a fine Jewish boy to have sport with. His kind, her kind. Only there was something wrong. Obviously a good lay, but inside thinking this was a way to reach life.

Where else to seek but from the men she had access to? She knew one individual man, her father. Jean saw him as a flat surface, no dimensions. He ate, he gambled, he never reached out except to touch her breasts once or twice, slyly to be sure. A loving fatherly gesture. Jean knew the man was on the make.

Rockaway 1924, a gaudy summer resort. Jean was there to take care of her older sister's child. The deserted beach was her retreat. The ocean was her saviour. She could see a great span of space. She was not aware of the beach or the waves touching the shore, retreating flirtatiously, only the horizon, the escape, no buffeting, no challenge, just space. Jean knew the loneliness, always knew it but did not recognize it, so when this beautiful young man came to sit by her, in the evening twilight with the beach deserted, he unknowingly joined her in her quest.

He was about twenty-five, curly hair, blue eyes, stocky build, good-looking. 'A pretty girl alone. How come?'

'Just watching,' Jean's voice was muted. The challenge had come – a young man was seeing her. Jean watched herself as a warmth crept over her body. Her dimples were showing. She thrust her body forward to accentuate the outline of her breasts. Jean was going to make it.

My mother's legacy to me was the story of her desire. She has left sexual trails for me, private messages, how she saw her breasts, how her body swelled with want. She has also left the record of her anger, her fury at herself and others for forgetting the connection between generosity and lust. She never knew who to blame for her sexuality, for the rape, because the voices around her said her hunger deserved punishment. Forty-second Street did not scare or repulse her. It reminded her of empty beds. My mother feared and hated the women who, from the comfort of their marriages, called her whore. But she also knew on her own body, carried in her soul, the scars of sexual abuse. My mother accepted the fact that desire had made her homeless.

One night about two months later he invited me to a party. I went with fear, not trusting the man I loved. Yes, I thought I was in love. You know the saying, when you have had one, you have had them all – well, that was what happened to me that night. He passes me on to his friends, three in all. I wonder to this day how many of these men, I am sure now successful, ever think of that night and the complete frustration they had? I did not move. I disconnected myself from my body, froze my mind. I was considered a lousy lay by the three. Were they cruel? They were young men who thought the world was theirs.

I went home. He took me to my door at six in the morning. Not a word did I say. My mother and father were waiting. My father started to call me all the vile words he knew in English. My mother quietly stated she controlled the children. She would mete out punishment if necessary and that would be the final word. When we were alone she asked me if I was all right, told me if I was pregnant I would not be alone, kissed me, and told me to go to bed. Never again was the incident brought up.

God did I need help.

I would not accept the tangibles, the penis, the vagina, as a way of life. Necessary yes. I treated the physical as the entree to the man as he entered me. Doctor, this one experience now haunts me and I seek the answer. Was I the victim or the stimulus of the event? That evening of the rape I came away still young, still desiring the beauty of a sexual relationship, frightened of words not being able to express the experience, afraid to admit that there existed in men such cruelty. I buried the truth. I lived the lie that men do not and cannot perpetuate evil. Love is all-pervasive. Cruelty does and did exist, but the people were sick. But in my life despair took over.

Doctor, I still believe the lie that human compassion, humble awareness is the only common sense.

Our love affairs collided as we grew older. Once when I needed your solace because I was losing a woman I loved deeply, I walked the eighty blocks between our apartments to find you sitting in your slip with your boss and lover, Mr Ulano. He sat across from you in his short sleeves and suspenders, in the formal intimate way I had come to know as your post-love-making demeanor. I could not speak to you then. Mother and daughter were each pursuing illicit loves. I never thought you saw my need of you but I was wrong.

June 27, 1970. I saw Joan today and it was a portent of all things to come. She was going to the coast for two months. Afraid to say good-bye, she called and said she didn't have time to see me. I wished her a good trip. She called five minutes later to tell me she would stop by for a very short time – a minute or so. So full of love and guilt, not knowing how I feel, speaking trivialities when my heart is screaming out to her, take care, take care. I love you my dearest. God, may she always see her way and not despair. Shedding her responsibilities, her work, headed like a child to her fun, knowing she deserved it. She removes herself when she thinks she will hurt. Can I show less courage and integrity than she? The daughter becomes the teacher, the mother the student.

Sometimes all we have to give each other is words. We hoped the cracks would not get deeper, but they did. The bosses never left their wives; they never solved my mother's financial problems. But at least the office where my mother lived most of her life was emotional territory, an erotic home where praise for business skill was given with a wink of appreciation for her sexual abilities. She diffused their power by fucking them. When she left, she made sure their books were in good order.

At some point in the early fifties, it all began to drift away. The weekly subpoenas would be jammed into her bag, unopened. I lived waiting for the legal explosions; they came but they never blew her entirely away, just piece by piece.

In 1958, when she discovered me in bed with a woman lover, she gave me an ultimatum – leave the house or see a doctor. She knew seeing a doctor was not going to be my choice. She kicked me out of the house and I became part of the torrent of the sixties; it was the right time for me. I could use all she had taught me, all I had witnessed: my anger at bosses, at the finger-waggers who called her whore, at the secure who flourished in streets of pain, at bigots who locked restaurants and school buildings. My queerness rode with me on Freedom Rides, walked the miles between Selma and Montgomery, helped swell the ranks of the peace marches, protested the shelter drills, sat with me in front of the House Un-American Activities Committee as we applauded an exhausted Joanne Grant while one of the senators called us scum of the earth. And while I marched and chanted, my mother worked day by day to keep herself alive.

December 29, 1969. I'm drunk. I'm listening to the hilarious news on television. More draftees, more killings, more injustice. I can't hold on much longer. Is it my own unhappiness? I am not as holy as I wish to think. I hate the man I love. I hate myself for loving him. I hate his values, his estimation of who you are, how good is your credit, how much money do you have. I have no money, no position. I live week by week, salary by salary, hate my work, hate what kept me alive. I could have gone on if I was able to give and receive love. So, you say, what the hell do you want? So I didn't get it. So I didn't deserve it. So I didn't play the game. So they didn't play my game. Only fucking, literally and figuratively, is the whole game. Do it well and you will be a success, do it with your heart and call it love, be sure you will get a good fucking. I am sick of my body demanding the touch of love, sick to my soul of all the ugliness.

Come on Youth, fight with all your weapons. Save this world for yourselves. We have only garbage. I am part of it. Dump us, burn us, but don't become one of us. Be humble to your own. Give yourselves love; we won't recognize it.

I had to wean myself away from expecting love administered in the custom of the families around me. My mother never taught me how to be a lady, how to brush my teeth or the right way to wipe myself. She never passed on recipes or fashion hints or her favorite brand of lipstick. She never told me to get married or to go college. She did pay a man to fuck me to see if I was a Lesbian. She was drunk when she arranged it, but I think she was not ashamed of her attempt. She needed to know if I, too, could be a good lay. I was, Regina, with the women who made me feel beautiful. She taught me how to search out live nit eggs that clung to the bottom of my hair and crack their bodies between my nails. She taught me laughter and endurance and the right to passion. She taught me the absurdity of power when it is used on the powerless.

December 29, 1969. I was born, given a name, parents – made the best of it. I was a wife who could not follow the beaten path, always hungering for an answer. I was a mother, a sick mother, but a mother. I gave birth. The physical event was not important, but I loved another human being. Not the right outlook for a mother, so I loused that up. But by God I love these adults, not because I am a mother, but I see them struggling to gain identity.

Regina the woman: who the hell is she? In bed, terrific, so I am told. A good lay is still a good lay regardless of what causes the good fucking. How lonely is all the playacting. What do I need to make me whole?

What do I do with this legacy – a mother who wills me her views on fucking, her despair, her outrage? Her rebellion out-lasted those of Abbie Hoffman, Jerry Rubin, and Eldridge Cleaver. She just got tired. The days of work did not stop, and she was no longer the boss' best friend. Elliot and I started getting telephone calls. 'Bail me out. I need money. Come get me.' She would go for long periods without telling us where she was working. Then I would get a frantic call from Miriam, her twin sister, asking me if it was true mother was a prostitute. When the calls from her finally came, they showed me worlds of humiliation in which she had learned to survive: the residential hotel that evicted her, where my lover and I had to rescue her clothes. I introduced myself as Regina's daughter and they told me to wait outside. They wheeled out a dirty laundry bin, trailing her stockings and underwear, on the street. We scooped up handfuls of her clothes and stuffed them into suit-cases. The tape recorder I had given her to help with her writing had disappeared.

Soon the trail she left behind grew smaller and smaller. Each eviction pared away her possessions. The final time I picked up her pieces was in the green-walled basement of the hospital where they had put her suitcase and found myself touching her shit. My last gift to her, a green bathrobe, covered with her final fear. They had carefully placed it in a plastic bag and laid it on top of her writings. For one moment, the whole world smelled of shit and then I realized it was only the bathrobe, and I threw it in a garbage can.

An Open Letter to My Children, 1969. You, my son, visit the neighborhood, the apartment house, peer through mailboxes looking for familiar names, looking for your innocence, your dreams. Do not let memories dim the present or the future.

You, my daughter, love yourself, you are worthy. Bear no guilt. Out of sorrow you have created love and compassion.

I, too, sought the old home, saw two small children look at me with confidence and love. I see you both and now I see the present, the anger that shields your love, my life entwined with yours, part of the memories. Now that you are both grown and I am in the deep middle age of life, I know that we are richer for all our hurts. What you will be will encompass all memories, we three who love each other very much.

From the Lesbian Activist section of the *Gay Activist Alliance Newsletter*, April 1973:

> 'Blessed Be the Mothers of the Lesbian Nation' Feb. 4, 1973, marked, perhaps, the beginning of a new stage in the Lesbian movement. The Lesbian Liberation Committee sponsored a panel called 'Mothers of Lesbians' which proved to be one of the most exciting and hopeful Lesbian discussions presented at the Firehouse, to date. Joan Nestle's mother made a very moving statement about Joan as a person: a beautiful person whose choices could only be good ones.

Twice my mother stole from her bosses, once out of desperation and the second time out of terror. When she stole for herself, she stole badly and was caught both times. By now, my mother's world was slipping away. She couldn't control the numbers or the men anymore, but she fought back with all the magic of her bookkeeper's language:

Oct. 15, 1976

Mr Brenner:

I received the subtle threat addressed to my children, with regards to my misdeeds, which, incidentally, you were aware of as far back as two-and-a-half years ago. I did not at any time cover or manipulate your books to hide the deficit. I am not pleading my cause, as a matter of fact, part of my healing is admitting to 'improper behavior' – but for you to assume a holier-than-thou moral judgment is laughable. The powerful have the right, your philosophy?

Now to the settlement of the debt. There are discrepancies and I shall enumerate: According to my records, the $800.00 given back to you from my bonus seems not to be credited to my account. I may be in error and the only way this can be proven is to send copies of my earning sheets of 1974 and 1975, showing deductions from my income to be credited to indebtedness and judgments against my salary. As to the

$60.00 for dresses that you list, I paid this sum to your former colleague, Johnnie, you remember him, your disposer of checks. I am being sardonic and humorous, poor soul. He thought he had it made. Don't we all, including you. I am sure I am not intimidating you, and it is not my style, as I am accountable for my actions as you are for yours and I do believe in justice. However, you better believe that all correspondence now or in the future directed to my children shall possibly be a heartache to you. My sins are mine, period.

I am enclosing, herewith, a money order for $75.00 which you will be receiving every month until the indebtedness is paid, but I must insist upon receiving the papers requested. In the event you do not accept these terms, I shall return to New York and you shall determine your method of justice and I shall pursue mine.

Now even the dresses must be accounted for. No longer does your body soften the edge between the boss and you. You use the language of business, it *herewiths* and *the aboves*, to fight desperate battles. I also fight back on your behalf, tired of the years I had to be a good girl in front of the bosses.

September 17, 1976

Dear Mr Brenner:

I am sending you my mother's address but first I want to say some things. My mother helped in paying back the $3100. She is now living on social security with my brother in California. My mother has worked her whole life primarily for one thing – to raise her children with dignity. She did this alone, working in small rooms, taking care of the bosses' books. The years of loneliness and frustration did not produce an always sensible, 'rational' woman. When she committed those 'improper actions', she was ill – ill with a life of struggle and loneliness. The money went to a man who regularly threatened to kill her. I look at my mother now and I love her. Sometimes she is 'crazy', but she has worked a lifetime in a business world that never saw her as an important person, in a man's world where she serviced her bosses – lied for them, cheated for them, saved on taxes, off the books, on the books. I don't know if this letter makes sense to you, but I had to write it. Much more was taken from my mother than she ever took. Someday the world will be different. Profits and business will not be based on the lives of less powerful people – particularly women. My mother has my everlasting honor and respect.

'I am not a mother', she would say. 'I am Regina, a woman.' Always, always that would be her cry, and when she came to me for money I did not have, or because her lovers brutalized her, or when she lost a job, I wanted to cry, 'But mother, I am not a daughter, just a woman. Please leave me alone.'

I don't know when my mother started gambling, but the race-track and later OTB were as necessary to her as lovemaking. Driven by loneliness, my mother pushed herself into unwomanly territory. She rode the lonely people's bus, scrawled her figures on any available piece of paper in her purse, usually lost. She stood in small gatherings feeling the warmth of nightly comrades around her, people like herself who needed to win and should have won and yet who knew that just being there they were already losers. Sometimes she took me, but I hated it all. All I saw was Regina surrounded by shabby men. Regina being an expert, once again using magic numbers to win warmth, and always, it seemed to me, Regina losing. I watched with fury as rent money disappeared under the grill, transformed into small dull tickets like the thousand others scattered on the stained cement floor. I thought my mother's money should be spent on food and shelter. I did not know her fury at the money she was forced to make, her refusal to accept the tedium of her life by doing the right things with it. In her last year, she would flee the apartment Deborah and I had furnished for her to the OTB store across Broadway. She would stand there, cradling her pocketbook under her arm, in a light blue coat, a small woman once again surrounded by men.

The bus awaits, the program is bought, away we go to glory or to doom. It doesn't matter. We are where the action is, the comradeship, the sympathetic ear, the boast of winning the day before. We look at each other almost lovingly. We all protest we are not compulsive gamblers, but we do not confess the need for ties that have meaning. We are not missed anyplace, are on the bus because we have no other place to go. The prostitute is there to reap from men their rejuvenated masculinity. The women no one needs is there hoping for a crumb of attention. Maybe she will be acknowledged as a good tipster. There is no sex.

We reach the bus, the evening over. Some think about the lonely trip, what the hell am I doing here, others hate themselves and hate the world, others boast of their winning and hurt their comrades. All agree it is a crooked game.

Of all of it, it was your loneliness I could bear least: you who wanted touch so much became so diminished in your passions. I always saw you coming home from work so tired, so burdened. I wanted desperately to be able to call in from the other room your young husband full of strength and safety. Then, as I grew older, I wanted you to accept the love of women. Finally I wanted you to accept my love. But you did things your own way, like a tenacious farmer chopping earth away from stone.

I met him on a bus coming home from the track. I was terribly depressed, not because of losing, but from the sheer terror of spending an evening without any personal contact. He sat down beside me, even though there were many empty seats. Casually glancing at him, I got the impression of a man in his middle forties, a strong-featured man with a brooding face, hunched shoulders, a big man. He asked me how I made out. I told him indifferently that I had lost a little. The conversation became desultory until I heard him say he had just returned from

85

Vietnam. I reacted immediately, wanted to know more. I found out he was on a warship delivering war materials. On hearing his version of the war, I dubbed him a reactionary but what the hell, he was somebody to talk to. We got off the bus at Forty-second Street. He indifferently asked me if I would care to have a drink. We went to a bar across from where I lived and I proceeded to get cockeyed drunk. Left myself wide open for what-ever would happen. Do I sound unemotional about it all? Did I know this man was to offer me a challenge? Yes I knew from the beginning. I knew he was a loner. I knew he needed human contact, but so did I. Thinking that I could help myself by reaching out, I reached out, loaded, angry, crying. I brought him up to my apartment. We clung together. I fell asleep in his arms, not knowing his name, not caring.

I remember the night in Flushing when you came home drunk. We were all waiting for you: Uncle Jack, your most devoted boyfriend; Mabel, waiting to be paid after a long day of work; Susan, my first woman lover; and myself. You came in stag-gering and saw us all staring at you with worry. You started throwing money at us, shouting that was all Regina was good for, that was all we wanted you for. You collapsed on the couch and when I bent over you, you grabbed my arm and started kissing it, feverishly telling me I was the only one who under-stood. Susan ran out the door, frightened by the chaos. Mabel told me, 'Go after your woman, I'll take care of Regina.' I did. I fled from the knowledge that you hated me for being another waiting face and that you loved me for being the one closest to your torment.

   I started work at thirteen and I never took money from you, but I wished it was not me that you had to come home to. When I walked in countries you had never seen, had years of peace with Deborah my lover that Jonas did not live long enough to give you, I measured my freedoms against your servitude. The day before you died I told you you would not have to work anymore. You called Rose, your enduring friend, to tell her that your children had freed you.

May 7, 1977

Joan Dear,

*Your birthday – my celebration of the beautiful gift I
received on Mother's Day thirty-seven years ago – when I
held you in my arms and you were not more than three
hours old and you looked up at me with your glorious
blue eyes. They did not wander or flitter as most babies do.
The bond was made and if it seems, at times, the
communication is weak, the compelling tie of love and
devotion, recognition, strength was there.*

*My love is so great that to see you face to face I would
become 'emotional'. Just today I want to say that for
always your love has been my greatest gift – you made me
a beautiful person in my eyes for which I say thank you for
being my daughter.*

December 22. 1978. Mother, today I brought you Colette and
Willa Cather whom you wanted to read, but I knew you would
not be able to. You are lying on your deathbed, plugged into small
television screens that record in orange lines when your heart
bleeds or screams or stops. Since Tuesday you have been a
captured woman. When I was very small, lying in a hospital bed,
scared and wanting you there all the time, I remember
you standing above me, dressed for business, a working woman
who could not miss a day. You looked down at me and said, 'Don't
worry, I'll be here.' Later, when you thought I was sleeping, you
called your boss to apologize for being late and to say you would
be in soon. We both knew you could not stay.

Now I cannot see you. You lie in the most critical bed – a place
of honor. I see down the long blue corridor. Yellow lights shine at
the end and white coats swing as they go in and out
of your room. You waited for me to get home from work before
you would accept the heart attack. You waited for your working
daughter. I found you dying, and now I go to work every day
before I come here. In every hour, I have ten minutes to
give you my love. Your eyes beg me for help. You are tired

and in pain. You write me a note: 'Death would be a treasure.' The machines are pumping at you, liquids are flowing in. The doctor turns down your stained sheet to show me the heart burns from electric shock, but all I can see is your pink nipple.

Butch-Femme Relationships:
Sexual Courage In The 1950s

$\mathbf{F}$or many years now, I have been trying to figure out how to explain the special nature of butch-femme relationships to Lesbian-feminists who consider butch-femme a reproduction of heterosexual models. My own roots lie deep in the earth of this Lesbian custom, and what follows is one Lesbian's understanding of her own experience.

In the late 1950s I walked the streets looking so butch that straight teenagers called me a bulldyke; however, when I went to the Sea Colony, a working-class Lesbian bar in Greenwich Village, looking for my friends and sometimes for a lover, I was a femme, a woman who loved and wanted to nurture the butch strength in other women. I am now forty years old (1981). Although I have been a Lesbian for over twenty years and I embrace feminism as a world view, I can spot a butch thirty feet away and still feel the thrill of her power. Contrary to belief, this power is not bought at the expense of the femme's identity. Butch-femme relationships as I experienced them, were complex erotic statements, not phony heterosexual replicas. They were filled with a deeply Lesbian language of stance, dress, gesture, loving, courage, and autonomy. None of the butch women I was with, and this included a passing woman, ever presented themselves to me as men; they did announce themselves as tabooed women who were willing to identify their passion for other women by wearing clothes that symbolized the taking of responsibility. Part of this responsibility was sexual expertise. In the 1950s this courage to feel comfortable with arousing another woman became a political act.

Butch-femme was an erotic partnership serving both as a conspicuous flag of rebellion and as an intimate exploration of women's sexuality. It was not an accident that butch-femme couples suffered the most street abuse and provoked more assimilated or closeted Lesbians to plead with them not to be so obvious. An excerpt from a letter by Lorraine Hansberry, published in the Ladder[1] in 1957, shows the political implications of the butch-femme statement. The letter is a plea for discretion because, I believe, of the erotic clarity of the butch-femme visual image.

> Someday I expect the 'discrete' lesbian will not turn her head on the streets at the sight of the 'butch' strolling hand in hand with her friend in their trousers and definitive hair-cuts. But for the moment it still disturbs. It creates an impossible area for discussion with one's most enlightened (to use a hopeful term) heterosexual friends.[2]

A critic of this essay has suggested that what was really the problem here was that 'many other Lesbians at that time felt the adoption of culturally defined roles by the butch-femme was not a true picture of the majority of Lesbians. They found these socialized roles a limiting reality and therefore did not wish to have the butch-femme viewpoint applied or expressed as their own.'[3]

My sense of the time says this was not the reason. The butch-femme couple embarrassed other Lesbians (and still does) because they made Lesbians culturally visible, a terrifying act for the 1950s. Hansberry's language – the words *discrete* and *definitive* – is the key, for it speaks of what some wanted to keep hidden: the clearly sexual implications of the two women together. The *Ladder* advocated a 'mode of behavior and dress acceptable to society,' and it was this policy Hansberry was praising. The desire for passing, combined with the radical work of survival that the *Ladder* was undertaking, was a paradox created by the America of the fifties. The writing in the *Ladder* was bringing to the surface years of pain, opening a door on an intensely private experience, giving a voice to an 'obscene' population in a decade of McCarthy witch hunts. To survive meant to take a public stance of societal cleanliness. But in the pages of the journal itself, all dimensions of Lesbian life were explored including butch-femme relationships. The *Ladder* brought off a unique balancing act for the 1950s. It gave nourishment to a secret and subversive life while it flew the flag of assimilation.

However, it was not the rejection by our own that taught the most powerful lesson about sex, gender, and class that butch-femme represented, but the anger we provoked on the streets. Since at times femmes dressed similarly to their butch lovers, the aping of heterosexual roles was not always visually apparent, yet the sight of us was enraging. My understanding of why we angered straight spectators so is not that they saw us modeling ourselves after them, but just the opposite: we were a symbol of women's erotic autonomy, a sexual accomplishment that did not include them. The physical attacks were a direct attempt to break into this self-sufficient erotic partnership. The most frequently shouted taunt was, 'Which one of you is the man?' This was not a reflection of our Lesbian experience as much as it was a testimony to the lack of erotic categories in straight culture. In the fifties, when we walked in the Village holding hands, we knew we were courting violence, but we also knew the political implications of how we were courting each other and chose not to sacrifice our need to their anger.[4]

The irony of social change has made a radical, sexual political statement of the 1950s appear today as a reactionary, nonfeminist experience. This is one reason I feel I must write about the old times – not to romanticize butch-femme relationships but to salvage a period of Lesbian culture that I know to be important, a time that has been too easily dismissed as the decade of self-hatred.

Two summers ago in Kansas at the National Women's Studies Association Conference, a slide show was presented to the Lesbian caucus in which a series of myths about Lesbians was entertainingly debunked. The show was to be used in straight sex-education classrooms. One of the slides was a comic representation of the 'myth' of butch-femme relationships with voiceover something like: 'In the past, Lesbians copied heterosexual styles, calling themselves butch and femme, but they no longer do so.' I waited until the end to make my statement, but I sat there feeling that we were so anxious to clean up our lives for heterosexual acceptance that we were ready to force our own people into a denial of some deep parts of their lives. I knew what a butch or femme woman would feel seeing this slide show, and I realized that the price for social or superficial feminist acceptance was too high. If we deny the subject of butch-femme relationships, we deny the women who lived them, and still do.

Because of the complexity and authenticity of the butch-femme experience, I think we must take another look at the term *role-playing*, used primarily to summarize this way of loving. I do not think the term serves a purpose either as a label for or as a description of the experience. As a femme, I did what was natural for me, what I felt right. I did not learn a part; I perfected a way of loving. The artificial labels stood waiting for us as we discovered our sexualities.

We labeled ourselves as part of our cultural ritual, and the language reflected our time in history, but the words which seem so one-dimensional now stood for complex sexual and emotional exchanges. Women who were new to the life and entered bars have reported they were asked: 'Well, what are you – butch or femme?' Many fled rather than answer the question. The real questions behind this discourse were, 'Are you sexual?' and 'Are you safe?' When one moved beyond the opening gambits, a whole range of sexuality was possible. Butch and femme covered a wide variety of sexual responses. We joked about being a butchy femme or a femmy butch or feeling kiki (going both ways). We joked about a reversal of expectations: 'Get a butch home and she turns over on her back.' We had a code language for a courageous world for

which many paid dearly. It is hard to re-create for the 1980s
what Lesbian sexual play meant in the 1950s, but I think it is
essential for Lesbian-feminists to understand, without shame,
this part of their erotic heritage. I also think the erotic for us, as
a colonized people, is part of our social struggle to survive and
change the world.

A year ago some friends of mine were discussing their experiences in talking about butch-femme relationships to a
women's studies class. Both had been gay since the 1950s and
were active in the early gay liberation struggles. 'I tried to
explain the complex nature of butch sexuality, its balance of
strength and delicacy,' Madeline said. 'The commitment to
please each other was totally different from that in heterosexual
relationships in which the woman existed to please the man.'

As she spoke, I realized that not only was there the erotic
statement made by the two women together, but there was and
still is a butch sexuality and a femme sexuality, not a woman-
acting-like-a-man or a woman-acting-like-a-woman sexuality,
but a developed Lesbian-specific sexuality that has a historical
setting and a cultural function. For instance, as a femme I
enjoyed strong, fierce love-making; deep, strong givings and
takings; erotic play challenges; calculated teasings that called
forth the butch-femme encounter. But the essential pleasure
was that we were two women, not masqueraders. When a
woman said, 'Give it to me baby!' as I strained to take more of
her hand inside of me, I never heard the voice of a man or of
socially conditioned roles. I heard the call of a woman world-
traveler, a brave woman, whose hands challenged every denial
laid on a woman's life.

For me, the erotic essence of the butch-femme relationship
was the external difference of women's textures and the bond
of knowledgeable caring. I loved my lover for how she stood as
well as for what she did. Dress was a part of it: the erotic signal
of her hair at the nape of her neck, touching the shirt collar;
how she held a cigarette; the symbolic pinky ring flashing as
she waved her hand. I know this sounds superficial, but all
these gestures were a style of self-presentation that made

erotic competence a political statement in the 1950s. A deep partnership could be formed with as many shared tasks as there are now and with an encouragement of the style which made the woman I loved feel most comfortable. In bed, the erotic implications of the total relationship only became clearer. My hands and lips did what felt comfortable for me to do. I did not limit my sexual responses because I was a femme. I went down on my lovers to catch them in my mouth and to celebrate their strength, their caring for me. Deeper than the sexual positioning was the overwhelming love I felt for their courage, the bravery of their erotic independence.

As a way of ignoring what butch-femme meant and means, feminism is often viewed as the validating starting point of healthy Lesbian culture. I believe, however, that many pre-Stonewall Lesbians were feminists, but the primary way this feminism – this autonomy of sexual and social identities – was expressed, was precisely in the form of sexual adventuring that now appears so oppressive. If butch-femme represented an erotically autonomous world, it also symbolized many other forms of independence. Most of the women I knew in the Sea Colony were working women who either had never married or who had left their husbands and were thus responsible for their own economic survival. Family connections had been severed, or the families were poorer than the women themselves. These were women who knew they were going to work for the rest of their Lesbian days to support themselves and the homes they chose to create. They were hairdressers, taxi drivers, telephone operators who were also butch-femme women. Their feminism was not an articulated theory; it was a lived set of options based on erotic choices.

We Lesbians from the fifties made a mistake in the early seventies: we allowed our lives to be trivialized and reinterpreted by feminists who did not share our culture. The slogan 'Lesbianism is the practice and feminism is the theory' was a good rallying cry, but it cheated our history. The early writings need to be reexamined to see why so many of us dedicated ourselves to understanding the homophobia of straight feminists rather than the life-realities of Lesbian women 'who were not feminists' (an empty phrase which comes too easily to the lips). Why did we expect and need Lesbians of earlier generations and differing backgrounds to call their struggle by our name? I am afraid of the answer because I shared both worlds and know how respectable feminism made me feel, how less dirty, less ugly, less butch and femme. But the pain and anger at hearing so much of my past judged unacceptable have begun to surface. I believe that Lesbians are a people, that we live as all people do, affected by the economic and social forces of our times. As a people, we have struggled to preserve our people's ways, the culture of women loving women. In some sense, Lesbians have always opposed the patriarchy; in the past, perhaps most when we looked most like men.

As you can tell by now, this essay is an attempt to shake up our prevailing judgments. We disowned the near-past too quickly, and since it was a quiet past – the women in the Sea Colony did not write books – it would be easy not to hear it. Many women have said to me, 'I could never have come out when you did.' But I am a Lesbian of the fifties, and that world created me. I sit bemused at Lesbian conferences, wondering at the academic course listings, and I know I would have been totally intimidated by the respectability of some parts of our current Lesbian world. When Monique Wittig said at the Modern Language Association Conference several years ago, 'I am not a woman, I am a Lesbian,' there was a gasp from the audience, but the statement made sense to me. Of course I am a woman, but I belong to another geography as well, and the two worlds are complicated and unique.

The more I think of the implications of the butch-femme world, the more I understand some of my discomfort with the customs of the late 1970s. Once, when the Lesbian Herstory Archives presented a slide show on pre-1970 Lesbian images, I asked the women how many would feel comfortable using the word *Lesbian* alone without the adjunct *feminism*. I was curious about the power of the hyphenated word when so few women have an understanding of the Lesbian 1950s. Several of the women could not accept the word *Lesbian* alone, and yet it stood for women who did stand alone.

I suggest that the term *Lesbian-feminist* is a butch-femme relationship, as it has been judged, not as it was, with *Lesbian* bearing the emotional weight the butch does in modern judgment and *feminist* becoming the emotional equivalent of the stereotyped femme, the image that can stand the light of day. Lesbianism was theory in a different historical setting. We sat in bars and talked about our lives; we held hands in the streets and talked about the challenge of knowing what we were not permitted to do and how to go beyond that; we took on police harassment and became families for each other. Many of us were active in political change struggles, fed by the energy of our hidden butch-femme lives which even our most liberal-left friends could not tolerate. Articulated feminism added another layer of analysis and understanding, a profound one, one that felt so good and made such wonderful allies that for me it was a gateway to another world – until I realized I was saying *radical feminist* when I could not say *Lesbian*.

My butch-femme days have gifted me with sensitivities I can never disown. They make me wonder why there is such a consuming interest in the butch-femme lives of upper-class women, usually the more removed literary figures, while real-life, working butch and femme women are seen as imitative and culturally backward. Vita Sackville-West, Jane Heap, Missy, Gertrude Stein, and Radclyffe Hall are all figures who shine with audacious self-presentation, and yet the reality of passing women, usually a working-class Lesbian's method of survival, has provoked very little academic Lesbian-feminist interest.

Grassroots Lesbian history research projects are beginning to change this, however. The San Francisco Lesbian and Gay Men's History Research Project has created a slide show called '. . . And She Also Chewed Tobacco,' which discusses passing women in San Francisco at the turn of the century. The Buffalo Lesbian Oral History Project (Madeline Davis and Liz Kennedy) is focusing on the lives of pre-1970 working-class Lesbians.* The Lesbian Herstory Archives of New York has a slide show in progress called 'Lesbian Courage, Pre-1970' and there are groups in Boston, Washington, DC, and Philadelphia attempting to be more inclusive of the Lesbian experience.

Because I quickly got the message in my first Lesbian-feminist CR group that such topics as butch-femme relation-ships and the use of dildoes were lower class, I was forced to understand that sexual style is a rich mixture of class, history, and personal integrity. My butch-femme sensibility also incor-porated the wisdom of freaks. When we broke gender lines in the 1950s, we fell off the biologically charted maps. One day many years ago, as I was walking through Central Park, a group of cheerful straight people walked past me and said, 'What shall we feed it?' The *it* has never left my consciousness. A butch woman in her fifties reminisced the other day about when she was stoned in Washington Square Park for wearing men's clothes. These searing experiences of marginality because of sexual style inform my feminism.

Butch-femme women made Lesbians visible in a terrifyingly clear way in a historical period when there was no Movement protection for them. Their appearance spoke of erotic indepen-dence, and they often provoked rage and censure both from their own community and straight society. Now it is time to stop judging and to begin asking questions, to begin listening. Listening not only to words which may be the wrong ones for the 1980s, but also to gestures, sadnesses in the eyes, gleams of victories, movements of hands, stories told with self-dismissal yet stubbornness. There is a silence among us, the voices of the 1950s, and this silence will continue until some of us are ready to listen. If we do, we may begin to understand how our Lesbian people survived and created an erotic heritage.

* To be published under the title, *Boots of Leather, Slippers of Gold.*
It took me forty years to write this essay. The following women helped make it possible: Frances Taylor, Naomi Holoch, Eleanor Batchelder, Paula Grant, and Judith Schwarz, as well as the *Heresies 12* collective, especially Paula Webster, who said 'do it' for years. Most deeply I thank Deborah Edel, my butchy Lesbian feminist former lover who never thought I was a freak.

Notes

1. The *Ladder*, published from 1956 to 1972, was the most sustaining Lesbian cultural creation of this period. As a street femme living on the Lower East Side, I desperately searched newspaper stands and drugstore racks for this small slim journal with a Lesbian on its cover. A complete set is now available at the Lesbian Herstory Archives in New York.

2. The *Ladder*, No. 1, May 1957, p. 28.

3. Letter from Sandy DeSando, August 1980.

4. An article in *Journal of Homosexuality* (Summer 1980), 'Sexual Preference or Personal Styles? Why Lesbians are Disliked' by Mary Reige Laner and Roy H. Laner, documented the anger and rejection of 511 straight college students toward Lesbians who were clearly defined as butch-femme. These results led the Laners to celebrate the withering away of butch-femme styles and to advocate androgyny as the safest road to heterosexual acceptance, a new plea for passing. This is the liberal voice turned conservative, the frightened voice that warns Blacks not to be too Black, Jews not to be too Jewish, and Lesbians not to be too Lesbian. Ironically, this advice can become the basis for a truly destructive kind of role-playing, a self-denial of natural style so the oppressor will not wake up to the different one in his or her midst.

Voices From Lesbian Herstory

To live without history is to live like an infant, constantly amazed and challenged by a strange and unnamed world. There is a deep wonder in this kind of existence, a vitality of curiosity and a sense of adventure that we do well to keep alive all of our lives. But a people who are struggling against a world that has decreed them obscene need a stronger bedrock beneath their feet.

We need to know that we are not accidental, that our culture has grown and changed with the currents of time, that we, like others, have a social history comprised of individual lives, community struggles, and customs of language, dress, and behavior – in short, that we have the story of a people to tell. To live with history is to have a memory not just of our own lives but of the lives of others, people we have never met but whose voices and actions connect us to our collective selves.

Having a history may be harder than not having one: this reality of continuity in time carries with it its own burdens. We will be in trouble if we act as Lesbians in the eighties as if the fifties or the twenties never existed. Because of the work of grassroots national and international Lesbian and gay historians, we have found patterns both in our oppression and in our responses. We can begin to analyze what went wrong and what went right. We are able to record the birth of new ways and to watch the dying of old ones. History makes us, at one and the same time, part of a community and alone as we watch the changes come. Having a history will certainly complicate the issues because simplistic positions will seldom do justice to it.

I am forty-two years old (1982), and I came out in 1958. I have made this statement many times before, but only now am I beginning to understand my own historical complexity. As I watch and participate in the Lesbian community now, I have many echoes in my head. I hear the voices of other times, and they have taught me important lessons. I celebrate and mourn at the same time. I want to tell you about what my past has taught me and about the challenges facing us today.

The Lesbian community is at a crossroads: we can either betray ourselves or carry our courage, culture, and intelligence into new territory. The recent raid on Blues, a Black Lesbian and gay men's working-class bar in Manhattan; the harassment of the Déjà Vue and the Duchess, two New York City Lesbian bars; the police attacks on Black Lesbians in Washington Square Park; the increased physical assaults on Lesbians and gay men in all parts of the country; the renewed arrests on Long Island of men wearing women's clothing; the refusal to give S/M Lesbian women space to talk and explore their sexuality; the hostility towards butch-femme Lesbians – all of these bring back to me the first layer of my history: the memory of being a queer, my inheritance from the fifties.

This is the layer of memory that makes me feel most lonely. The word *queer* is seen as a male word, or is so removed from the liberating energies of Lesbian-feminism that it makes me feel like a relic from another time just to use it. But I need the wisdom of that memory now. I need to remember what it was like to walk the streets as a young femme with my butch lover. I need to to remember what it was like to fight for sexual territory in the time of Joseph McCarthy. I need to remember the humiliation and the courage of standing on the bathroom line. I need to remember the flashing red lights that signaled police visits and the closed faces of the vice squad, the paddy wagons carrying off my friends. I need to keep alive the memory of passing women and their wives, the memory of Lesbians who because they 'looked like men' were ridiculed, beaten, locked up, hidden away. These women presented gender challenges at a time when only the deviants questioned gender destiny. I need to keep alive the memory that in the 1940s doctors measured the clitorises and nipples of Lesbians to prove our biological strangeness. When transvestites and transsexuals are beaten by the police, as they were at Blues, this history calls me to action. I cannot turn away from it. My roots lie in the history of a people who were called freaks.

The eighties, a more enlightened time, also have a message about being different. In a 1981 article in the *Journal of Homosexuality*, 'Sexual Preference or Personal Style: Why Are Lesbians Disliked' two well-meaning sociologists documented the anger of more than five hundred straight students, male and female, at Lesbians who are clearly butch-femme identified. These are the Lesbians found most objectionable by the survey's straight participants. The authors' closing advice is if Lesbians want greater heterosexual acceptance, they should adopt an androgynous style. I know this bargain, and it is a killing one. We are offered respectability if we 'tone down' our Lesbian selves; we are offered safety if we separate ourselves from the easily recognizable other. I see and hear the fear of being recognized as a queer every time we use the word *woman* when we know we really mean *Lesbian*. But I know queer women. I know their power and their courage, as well as their loneliness and their pain.

From 'Memories' by Jeanne Flash Gray in *The Other Woman* (vol. 1, no. 1), writing about Harlem gay life in the thirties and forties:

'Before it was discovered by others that Black Lesbians and gay men had money to spend, there were many places in Harlem run by and for Black Lesbians and gay men. When we were still bulldaggers and faggots . . . I am glad I had a chance to go to Blind Charlie's and Mr Rivers and similar places in Harlem. I am glad I had a chance to be a Bull Dagger before it became fashionable to be a Lesbian.'

From a letter documenting the early history of the Moody Garden Gang, a butch-femme working-class Lesbian community in Lowell, Massachusetts. The words belong to Jean, the lead guitarist and singer of an all-women's band that entertained in the late fifties and early sixties:

'When I was asked to play at the Silver Star Cafe in the fifties, there wasn't a place around for gay people and the few friends you had found to get together, and there was always the fear of being asked to leave a bar or being physically hurt when you left the bar at night. But here was a chance to be myself and be accepted for what I was. We started playing Friday, Saturday, and Sundays, all day, and within a short time, you had to be there early to get a seat. The kids poured in, and even though it still was a straight bar, we outnumbered the straights four to one and sometimes more than that. They came from all around, some traveling for two or three hours just for an evening with us. It was our Mecca, we were family, and we had found a home . . . So many of the kids ask what's so special about Moody Gardens. To us it was our world, a small world, yes, but if you were starving you didn't refuse a slice of bread, and we were starving just for the feeling of having others around us. We were kings of the hill. We were the *Moody Gardens*. And today the phrase Moody Gardens is as much a part of our lives as it was then. There isn't a person today that was part of that era that doesn't remember the good times and the bad, the friends that even after thirty years still take time to come together and remember. We are a small part of our history, and that's why I have to write and tell our sisters of today that if there hadn't been little Moody Gardens all over the world, we wouldn't even be allowed to get together as we do today and feel, in a small way, we are being accepted and we are not alone.'

New York City, 1927:

The first play on Broadway with a Lesbian theme is closed by the New York City vice squad for being immoral. Cast members and producers are arrested. A coalition of women's and church groups spearhead the campaign against this play and several others in New York and New Jersey that have gay sexuality as their themes.

New York City, 1962 (from Beebo Brinker, a Lesbian paperback written by Ann Bannon):*

'A rash of raids was in progress on the homosexual bar hangouts at the moment, with cops hustling old dykes who were village fixtures for eons off the streets so they wouldn't offend young middle-class wives.'

New York City, 1964:

Forty-six Lesbians are arrested in the largest raid on a Lesbian bar in New York City.

December 1971:

The United States Supreme Court rules that photographs showing explicit Lesbian sexual activity, including embracing, are obscene and therefore pornographic.

Toward the middle of the sixties I began to see clearly that besides being a queer, I was also a Lesbian. I was part of a special tradition and culture. That culture often brought me into conflict with another history I shared, that of being a woman. It wasn't until the early seventies that I learned the vocabulary of feminism and recognized, in another way, what I had always loved and admired in older Lesbians I had met:

*Reissued in 1983 by Naiad Press.

their audacity to be their own women, their brave dependence on no one but themselves for economic survival, their courage to have sexual expertise and to offer it to other women, their creation of women-loving communities in their homes and neighborhoods, their communal support of each other in times of illness, separation, and death. I had known a feminist community before I heard the clear enunciation of the ideology.

Feminism is now as essential to my history as is my Lesbianism – it is a way of viewing the world that challenges every traditional assumption about women. I have watched language change as women refuse to be historically trapped in old paradigms, old schemes of life that limit and distrust the power of women. I have been healed by women who are in search of old wisdoms, who have learned to understand their need for new sources of spiritual strength. I see the concrete struggle of feminists, Lesbian and straight, to challenge the physical brutalization of women that haunts all societies. Rape crisis centers, battered women's shelters, information hot-lines are all creations of the seventies, when feminism and Lesbianism joined hands.

All women's lives are precious, but histories are complicated things. While all Lesbian history is women's history, not all women's history is Lesbian history. These identities may be intertwined at times, but they are separate, distinct legacies, and at other times they may be in conflict.

From a letter dated January 10, 1927, written by a woman visitor to a meeting of the Heterodoxy Club, a group of feminists who met regularly in Greenwich Village:*

'One thing interested me or rather bothered me terribly in that meeting. I wonder whether you noticed it – or whether it was all my imagination. It was the woman who sat two

---

*See *The Radical Feminists of Heterodoxy* by Judith Schwarz (New Victoria Publishers, Norwich, Vermont, 1986).

places to the left of Dr. Hollingsworth. I think her name was
Helen Hull. It seemed to me that she had gone through a hell
of a life when she was younger. When Dr. Hollingsworth
included in her definition of the perfect feminist a woman
happily married and with children, it shattered all Miss
Hull's defense mechanisms. Did you notice how she turned
to the other psychoanalyst with white hair – Dr. Potter
wasn't it – and to one or two others and hoped they would
back her up and when they did not, did you see her face and
notice that she never spoke again? I wonder whether you
know anything about her. I may be a fool, but I think there
was a good deal of tragedy for her involved in that situation.'

In our time, the debate over sexuality has opened historical
wounds, wounds made even deeper by the fact that now it is
other Lesbians who are judging the acceptability of our sexuality. This is what my history has taught me:

If we choose to involve ourselves in the antipornography
movement, it would be helpful to keep in mind that many of us
were the early victims of vice squad raids, that some of us are
Lesbian prostitutes and sex workers, that we have a long
history of surviving and finding each other in places other
women were too frightened to walk through, that sexuality has
always been our frontier.

If we sign the NOW resolution against, among other things,
the public display of affection, we should remember that
others, like myself, made love in public bathrooms, on public
beaches, in parked cars, and in church pews, because we had
no other place to go, that Lesbians in the fifties were called
obscene for holding hands in public.

My Lesbian history tells me that the vice squad is never our
friend even when it is called in by women; that when police rid
a neighbourhood of 'undesirables' the undesirables have also
included street Lesbians; that I must find another way to fight
violence against women without doing violence to my Lesbian
self. I must find a way that does not cooperate with the state

forces against sexuality, forces that raided my bars, beat up my women, entrapped us in bathrooms, closed our plays, and banned our books.

Shame and guilt, censorship and oversimplified sexual judgments, the refusal to listen and the inability to respect sexual difference is not the world I have fought to create. The real challenge to all of us, Lesbians and feminists, is whether we can eliminate violence against women without sacrificing women's erotic complexities. I do not want to become a dictator of desire, not to other Lesbians and not to gay men who have the courage to listen to their own voices.

From a letter to the Lesbian Herstory Archives Newsletter written by Harriet Laine:

'I lived at home in 1960. (I was nineteen.) So did my lover. Sometimes we went to cheap hotels in the Times Square area, but often even this was hard to arrange. Somehow we heard of a woman on Fourteenth Street who rented out rooms to Lesbians by the hour or night (I no longer remember) and despite our terror of what we might find there, we went. The downstairs buzzer said Amazon Ltd on it. We were greeted at the door by a smiling woman who took us in the kitchen, made us some tea, and sat and talked with us for a while. Then she left us alone. The kitchen was at one end of a long hallway off of which there were several rooms. I guess these were the rooms she rented out, for we could sometimes hear muffled sounds coming from them. I don't remember ever actually seeing anyone else there. We never rented a room (still too afraid to acknowledge to someone else our erotic feelings), but we did go there frequently in that cold winter to sit and talk with her in the kitchen or by ourselves in the parlor room at the other end of the hallway. The woman, whose name I wonder if I ever knew, never asked for money or pressured us in any way. It was for us a safe space, and now I wonder about that woman and would certainly love to hear of anyone else who ever went there.'

One of the lessons I have learned in trying to live with history is that for every repression, we have found a suitable form of resistance. Our history is the chronicle of our vitality, our passion, our cunning, and at many times, our integrity. We must now work out a way by which we can honor both the old and the new. We must look for connections rather than judgments.

As we strive to uncover matriarchal myths, we must also keep in our minds the big-daddy tanks of our jails into which Lesbians who looked like men were thrown.

As we change our names to commemorate the earth, we must remember the women who changed their names to Frankie and Jo to commemorate their women-loving selves. And if we are tempted to dismiss them for being male-identified, we must reflect on how only the imprisoned know the kind of freedom they need the most.

While some of us may choose dress styles that clearly symbolize feminist fashion, we cannot judge the femme woman as either a victim or a traitor if she makes a visual gift of herself for the woman she loves and for her own pleasure.

While we look for the rituals of the Amazons, we should also explore the customs of Lesbian communities like the old Moody Garden Gang.

While we debate different sexual styles and their implications, we should never take from Lesbian women their right to explore and champion the sexuality they have won for themselves. We must not become our own vice squad by replacing the old word *obscene* with the new phrase *corrupted by the patriarchy.*

We can honor the women who fight violence against women by our dedication to creating more rape crisis centers and battered women's shelters. We can also honor the women who struggle to find new ways for us to explore sexual desire and fantasies. The creation of safe, open public sexual spaces for Lesbians is a much-needed political action.

In these days of Lesbian performers (or, as they call themselves, *women* performers) singing at Carnegie Hall, the wooing of us by national political parties, of big-budgeted gay civil rights organizations, remember that our battle is to be accepted in the fullness of our difference and not because we promise to be like everybody else.

As we explore women's culture and its connection to Lesbian culture, we must realize that we no longer have to say that being a Lesbian is more than a sexuality. Sexuality is not a limiting force but a whole world in itself that feeds the fires of all our other accomplishments. Many of us are just beginning to understand the possibilities of erotic choice and self-creation. It is this open declaration of our sexual selves that moralists and governments have tried to silence. They know that a Lesbian celebrating her desire is a symbol of the possibility of social change for all women.

Is it turning forty that makes me see layers of identities? I see the queer fifties, the Lesbian sixties, the feminist seventies, and it becomes clear to me that memory is something that goes beyond sequential incidents. None of these years have gone away, and none of the experiences are outdated; they, the wonderful jumble of them all, are the source of my politics, my work and my joy.

There are many other layers of our history that I have not touched on here: our individual ethnic and racial heritages, our class legacies, the community history of the differently abled, the history of Lesbian parenting, the long lineage of Lesbian cultural creators. They are all essential to our interpretation of our personal and communal experiences. They all may force painful choices at times, but with the conflict comes the glory – that we are all so many continuities at once.

Living with history may be burdensome, but the alternative is exile. We would never have the chance to embrace each other, to urge each other on in telling the whole story. We should not use history to stifle the new or to institutionalize the old; more it is a source of ideas, visions, tactics that constantly speak to us. The choice we make based on these voices and our own lives is the living gift we bequeath to our Lesbian daughters. Every present becomes a past, but caring enough to listen will keep us all alive.

My Mother Liked To Fuck

My mother, Regina, was not a matriarchal goddess or spiritual advisor. She worshipped at no altars and many times scorned the label mother. She was a Jewish working-class widowed woman who, from the age of fourteen, worked as a bookkeeper in New York's garment district. My father died before I was born, when my mother was twenty-nine, and left her with two children to raise. My mother liked sex and let me know throughout the years both the punishments and rewards she earned because she dared to be clear about enjoying fucking.

Regina was in my mind that October afternoon I sat in the front row of 1199's union auditorium to tape the panel discussion on pornography and eros. When my mother died, she left no money, no possessions, no property, no insurance policies. She left me only a sheaf of writings, scrawled letters and poems written on the back of yellow ledger sheets. I have written a longer piece about her and me incorporating these letters,* but for now I only want to talk about the courage of her sexual legacy and the sexual secrets I found in her writings and how she stood in my mind, the mind of her Lesbian daughter who has loved women for over twenty years, the afternoon of the panel.

At age thirteen my mother allowed herself to be picked up

---

* 'Two Women,' p. 78.

on a Coney Island beach and have sex with a good-looking Jewish young man who was in his twenties; three weeks later he invited her to his apartment where she was gang-raped by three of his friends. She became pregnant and had to have an abortion at age fourteen. The year was 1924. Her German father threatened to kill her, and she left school in the ninth grade to go to work. When my mother writes of these experiences she tells of her sexual passions, of how she wanted sex.

> I remember as a little girl, the impatience with my own youth. I recognized that I was someone, someone to be reckoned with. *I sensed the sexual order of life.* I felt its pull. I wanted to be quickly and passionately involved. God, so young and yet so old. I recognized my youth only in the physical sense, as when I exposed my own body to my own vision, saw the beautiful breasts, the flat stomach, the sturdy limbs, the eyes that hid sadness, needed love – a hell of a lot of grit and already acknowledging this to be one hell of a life. I was going to find the key. I knew the hunger but I did not know how to appease it.

She goes on to speak of her shock, pain, and hurt, and later of her anger at the rape, but she ends the narrative with a sexual credo: she would not let this ugliness take away her right to sexual freedom, her enjoyment of 'the penis and the vagina', as she puts it.

Respectable ladies did not speak to my mother for most of her widowed life. She picked up men at the racetrack, at OTB offices, slept with them, had affairs with her bosses, and generally lived a sexualized life. Several times she was beaten by the men she brought home. In her fifties, she was beaten unconscious by a merchant seaman when she refused to hand over her paycheck. My mother, in short, was both a sexual victim and a sexual adventurer; her courage grew as the voices of condemnation and threats of violence increased against her. I watched it all, and her belief in a woman's undeniable right to enjoy sex, to actively seek it, became a part of me. But I chose women. I wanted to kill the men who beat her, who took her week's pay. I wanted her not to need them and to come into my world of Lesbian friendship and passion, but she chose not to. We faced each other as two women for whom sex was important, and after initial skirmishes, she accepted my world of adventure as I did hers.

The week before she died, she was sexually challenging her doctor in the hospital, telling him he probably did it too quick for a woman like her. He, red-faced and young, drew the curtain around her hurriedly. At sixty-seven, my mother still wanted sex and made jokes about what she could do when she didn't have her teeth in. My mother was not a goddess, not a matriarchal figure who looms over my life big-bellied with womyn rituals. She was a working woman who liked to fuck, who believed she had the right to have a penis inside of her if she liked it, and who sought deeply for love but knew that it was much harder to find.

As Andrea Dworkin's litany against the penis rang out that afternoon, I saw my mother's small figure with her ink-stained calloused hands, never without a cigarette, held out toward me, and I saw her face with a slight smile.

So *nu*, Joan, is this the world you wanted me to have, where I should feel shame and guilt for what I like? I did for all the years of my life. I fought the rapist and the batterer and didn't give up my knowledge of what I liked. I looked at those dirty pictures, and I saw lonely people. Sometimes I did those things they do in dirty pictures, and wives would not speak to me. Their husbands fucked me first and then went home for *Shabbas*. I made lots of mistakes, but one thing I never did – I never allowed anyone to bully me out of my sexual needs. Just like you, Joan, when in the fifties I took you to doctors to see if you were a Lesbian, and they said you had too much hair on your face, you were a freak, and they never stopped you either. They called you freak and me whore and maybe they always will, but we fight them best when we keep on doing what they say we should not want or need for the joy we find in doing it. I fucked because I liked it, and Joan, the ugly ones, the ones who beat me or fucked me too hard, they didn't run me out of town, and neither can the women who don't walk my streets of loneliness or need. Don't scream *penis* at me, but help to change the world so no woman feels shame or fear because she likes to fuck.

Some Understandings

In these painful and challenging times, we must not run out on gay men and leave them holding the sexuality bag. It is tempting to some Lesbians to see themselves as the clean sex deviant, to disassociate themselves from public sexual activity, multiple partners, and intergenerational sex. While this may be the choice for some of us, it is not the reality of many others, not now and not in the past. Lesbian purity, a public image that drapes us in the cloak of monogamous long-term relationships, discreet at-home social gatherings, and a basic urge to re-create the family, helps no one. It does not do justice to either the choices it supposedly venerates or to our sexual indepen-dence. Long-term couples are often struggling with huge issues of lust and changes in sexual patterns. Discreet social gatherings were and often are the way close-knit sexual communities found a safe place to play. Public bathrooms have been social bedrooms for young Lesbians through the years who had no safe home to take their lovers back to, and we have long documented the lustful crushes of young Lesbians on older women, many more of which have been consummated than we encourage to be discussed.

Thus, by allowing ourselves to be portrayed as the good deviant, the respectable deviant, we lose more than we will ever gain. We lose the complexity of our own lives, and we lose what for me has been a lifelong lesson: you do not betray your comrades when the scapegoating begins. If, as Lesbians, we declare ourselves a people under attack for our sexual difference while at the same time we say, 'But we are not as different as they are,' then our assertion that we are victims of sexual judgment is self-serving. We cannot be sexual deviants only when it is safe to be so. Gay men, in large measure because of the onslaught of AIDS, are in danger of bearing the brunt of both private and public retaliations. We must not allow them to become isolated as a pubic sexual community. Historically, bigotry fueled by terror has led to mass exterminations of the offending human beings.

Another thorny issue that needs attention is the relationship between Lesbians and straight feminists. If we are to be comrades in the days of battle ahead, it is essential that we clear the air between us. The best way we can work together is suggested by some of the discussions in this book. I think the phrase, *every woman is a potential Lesbian,* is no longer useful. It trivializes my own history and the history of a community I was part of just as it trivializes the history of individual straight women. It once served a rhetorical purpose of carrying the discussion of Lesbian-feminism into more respectable places, but all my fifties knowledge tells me that my sexual journey was not a rhetorical device.

The police and the doctors and the red lights in the bars, the broken faces and the cruising cars full of hate, the head between my legs in a place I had never seen before and would never again, the leaving of homes to seek one's comrades in the streets, the pronoun deceptions used at work so that telephone calls to lovers would not label one a public freak, the flash of a knife in the hands of a mother who did not want her daughter to go out the door with a Lesbian – these were not the experiences of all women. So, too, I will never feel the push of childbirth, or endure the balancing act between autonomy and intimacy that many women are trying to work out in their relationships with men.

We must face each other knowing that we have made different choices, and that each choice opens us up to a different history. We each have an integrity of experience that can keep us from being the victims of our lives. This does not mean that I will ever accept lesbian-hating or disguised shame or sweeping heterosexual assumptions. The other part of the commitment, however, is to stop bullying women into sexual stances, to end the assumption that only Lesbians make choices.

We must stand together, realizing the complexity of our histories, both personal and social, choosing when we can tolerate each other's company and when we cannot. We must never pretend to be experts on each other's lives, never belittle the deep differences that do exist or pretend that we do not see the places of exposed pain.

I have dedicated my life to creating a memorial to the specialness of Lesbian lives, but so deeply do I know the way I have come that I can now join with comrades who are different, join to fight the terrors of coercive sex on the one hand and the dangers of state-regulated sex on the other. These two forces leave us a fragile piece of land in the middle, and it is on this territory that we must make our stand. It is the place where a woman's voice says simply, 'Touch me here because it feels good,' or 'Yes, I will take you now,' to whomever she chooses. Such a simple thing, and yet all the oppressions in the world conspire against it.

We must make our stand now as government and religious groups begin family preservation and sex reform campaigns. The headline 'Urge Sex Ed for JHS' can signal a new respect for teenage sexuality or an attempt to threaten and punish sexually active women. We must monitor these programs and even more importantly, we must start giving young women a forum to tell us what their sexuality means.

The battle for reproductive freedom is another one we must wage together to make sure that class and race do not determine who will be allowed to have sexual pleasure.

To even raise the issue of women's sexual freedom in the time of our government's invasion of Grenada may seem a bourgeois activity to some, but I have learned from the historical essays in this book (*Powers of Desire*) that times of governmental aggression set up a legacy of sexual repression for decades to come. Our government is now mobilizing this country for further assaults on governments it deems deviant. I believe that as celebrants of passion, we must become vocal antigovernment activists. When American rifles bring down the chosen governments of other countries, when bodies hit the earth never to rise again, what also dies with each one is their history of desire. If we do not battle as open sexual radicals fighting the forces of death, all the small freedoms we have won will disappear. These freedoms are crucial not only for this country but for all the countries of the world. In all its different cultural settings, the issue of women's sexual freedom will eventually become the test of how women are surviving in that culture.

Finally, to use the cadences of Frederick Douglass:

Until all women, young and old, black, red, yellow, and white, poor and middle class, gay and straight, have the power to announce and control their sexual pleasures, this struggle will go on.

Until all women have equal access to abortion, this struggle will go on.

Until all women are free from the terrors of physical and psychological abuse because they want to control their own destinies, this struggle will go on.

Until we have a government that uses compassion in the place of power, that recognizes a changed social order is the only way to stop the sufferings of the hungry, the homeless, the poor, the aged, the physically challenged, until we have a government that supports the freedom movements of the world and not the regimes that rule by hatred and police force, this struggle will go on.

Until the power of sexual joy has replaced the power of sexual fear, this struggle will go on.

This talk was delivered during an evening celebrating the publication of *Powers of Desire*, edited by Ann Snitow, Christine Stansell, and Sharon Thompson (Monthly Review Press, 1983).

The Gift Of Taking

I walk into the room. She stands with her back to me, a large woman dressed for business. She turns to me: 'I have been waiting.' I need to know my arrival is important to her. She approaches me. 'I will do what you want, I will do it better than you have ever had it done, and you will give me everything there is in you to give. You will pour it out on my hands, and I will hold you open.' I love her for those words, for her knowledge of what I need and her caring enough to do it. We are alone in this room, having left outside all our accomplishments, all our other powers.

Here we will face each other, naked and yet dressed in ritual recognition. We will have the courage to bring to the surface the messages the body carries from older days. Here the daily camouflage of acceptable activity will be dropped. My submission in this room with this woman is my source of strength, of wisdom. It informs all my abilities in the other world, but here I can give it time to breathe its own air, to break the surface and show its own face.

There is a table in the room with sharp square edges. It looks uncomfortable, but I long for the feel of its edges against my back.

I am wearing a long dress that hides my body, my body that I have hated so long for not being lean, hard; hated for its flesh, thighs without tight muscles, large buttocks mocked for many years but with a hunger all their own; and now yearning for penetration by this woman's hand, her erotic acceptance that will free me from the crime of being a big-assed woman. I know this woman, my friend, will bring my body to light, will make me use it and hear it, will strain it to its fullest, and she will help me through her demands and her pleasure to forget self-hatred. Through her gift of taking, I will be given back to myself, a self that must live in this body and thus desperately needs reconciliation.

'Come here, Joan.'

I do, my eyes caught on hers, a blush spreading fire on my face. 'You must be ready for me before I touch you. I want to feel your wetness waiting for me. You know that.' I do. She kisses me hard, her hands gripping my arms. The force of her tongue pushes my head back. She stands back and just looks at me. Her hands stay on me, and they will throughout our time together.

My breasts have grown hard and she knows it. She caresses my nipples, her eyes never leaving mine. 'I want them harder.' My body hears, and I feel flesh change its own form. Her fingers squeeze my nipples, but I do not drop my eyes. The pain is sweet; it destroys the years of numbness. I want her to squeeze harder. The message is exchanged in silence, and her hands take fuller command of my breasts. After a few minutes, I put my hand over hers to stop her giving. I can no longer hold my position.

'Now we will see.'

She holds my head back as she slips her hand under my dress. I tremble, trying to hold my thighs together, knowing she will not allow me. She feels the wetness before she touches my underpants. My thighs have seeped their own waters. Her hand forces my legs further apart and her fingers push aside the fabric. 'That is good, Joan,' she says, as my wetness bathes her fingers. She curves the material into a ribbon and pushes it between my cunt lips, gliding her thumbnail over the wet curve. 'You are a powerful woman, aren't you? Women listen to your words, and you do important work, but here you are in my hands.' Her hand spreads my lips apart.

'Yes, yes.'

She moves me closer to the table. She is ready to assume her full power, and I am ready to give to her. She holds me, undoes my dress. It falls open, and I feel the first shame of revelation, the fear she will turn away from me, from this body. 'Good,' she says. I hold on to her and close my eyes. I will not open them again until we are finished, but my hands will see her. I grip her shoulders, pulling her to me. She kisses me, deep, hard, forcing my mouth open. I take her tongue in, sucking on it, trying to hold it. She drops her head and sucks on my nipples, biting them. My nipples swell with fullness. She works harder. I know I will have marks to carry with me and I want them. I want to be reminded in the daily world of this breakthrough. The sweet soreness will burn through my heavy layers of work clothes and remind me of this need and this caring. I will blush with pleasure in the subway, or at a meeting, as a change in my body's position forces me to remember the time of openness.

Her hands are hard on me, and I want them to be. I hear her breath coming quicker and my own moaning breaking the silence. Her hands knead my belly, pushing my breath in and out. My hips move, I want her all inside of me. She pulls me back. For a brief moment I open my eyes. I can smell my sex in the room. 'Your body is bursting with want.'

'I know.' I can see it, hear it, smell it. My body is covered with a dark flush, and I am moving with want. I want to scream out to her, 'Now, please take me now,' but I can't, even in this dream. Perhaps next time I will be able to scream. I want to. I need to. For so many years I have not screamed, for so many years the world was not safe enough, or there was no one there to hear it.

I close my eyes again as she moves toward me. She speaks to me, always calling to me, challenging me, forcing me to be there, and the force of her tells me she is there, caring and fighting for me. Her lips move against my cheeks as she puts her hand on me. Her fingers tear away the fabric. She takes me into her hand, pushing, squeezing, opening. She slips one finger into me. I gasp at how she fills me with that one thrust when I have taken so much and will again, but still the first entry has all the joy, the surprise of her power. 'Open Joan, open, take me in. Maybe you can't. Maybe I'm too much for you.' I hold on to her tighter, open more, open to splitting to show her I can give a home to all she can give me. I can match her demanding with my giving, her hand with my insides. I speak to her through my muscles and my wetness. She moves in and out and I follow her. The table edge is cutting into my back as her weight pushes me over. She forces more fingers into me, and I feel as if I could take her whole hand, her arm. My hunger grows as she pushes against me, always talking to me, telling me she is there and wanting me.

I take her all in, throwing my whole body against her, repeating in a small deep voice. 'Yes, I can do it, I can do it.' Over and over again. She is a total force over me, and yet all her power is giving me myself. I know I am coming: all the need, the fear, the loneliness has slipped down around her fingers, and she pulls at them as she moves me. I am all in that place where her hand has found entrance.

I come on her fingers, contract and hold her inside of me. She feels me and whispers, 'There is more, I am not letting you go yet.' She moves around inside of me, making my body flinch with more comings. All my strength is in my hands, my arms embracing her strength, feeling her shoulder move with the power of her entries. I fall back on the table; my head drops back and she begins to leave me. I know it will not be easy. I have locked around her fingers, and she must carefully break the grip of my body's gratefulness.

When my strength returns, I will thank her by kneeling in front of her and taking her wetness in my mouth. I will hold her legs strong against me, my breasts holding her up, and I will slowly, carefully, wisely – using my tongue's tip and its wide surface and my teeth and the power of my mouth – give to her my love and her pleasure.

A Change Of Life

Her hair fell across my face, brown long curls that kept the moonlight from my eyes. I pushed it back and watched the light reclaim her face. 'Oh Joan,' she said, but I knew I would soon move from under her and with my hand wrapped in her hair, I would pull her down under me. I would move on her, waiting for her to beg me enter, and when I did, when I knew what this woman wanted, and when I undertook to give it to her as best as I could and as deep as I could for as long as I could, I would be answering all the desires I had ever had when I was on my back under the women who moved me.

'After forty, femmes turn butch,' we would repeat laughingly, young women in the bars. But the transformation seemed so far away, and we stood so hot in our pants, that this prediction was emptied of its cultural wisdom.

Now I am in my mid-forties, and for the first time I hold in my arms a woman who delights in her femininity, whose perfume I seek out, whose lipstick-lined lips make me melt for her, whose full body I want to hold with hands that are strong enough to leave their mark without losing their tenderness. I know her fears, they have been mine. I know her hungers, they have been mine. I know her delights, they have been mine.

Yet she is not me, not what I was or what I am. She is audacious in her femininity, in her flounces and swirls, in her long

tapered fingers and the bows at her neck. She is younger than I
by many years, just as the old stories said she would be. I have
become our own mythology. It has happened, a change of life
for at least the time I am with her.

My own body wants to be known only in the giving. I want
to come on top of her, moving my hips on her body, moving,
moving until I grow large and wet and then explode on her, my
wetness pouring out on her thighs, her belly, her cunt hair. I
keep my pants on, go barechested. I know I am trying to feel
like something other than the woman I usually am. I kneel
before her and slide my hand up her skirt, parting her legs,
finding her hidden warmth. My fingers slip in under the wet
panties and I find my home. She sits on the edge of the bed,
totally dressed, held by my thumb buried deep in her cunt. I
look up at her, watch her changing face as I rock her, push into
her until she must fall backward on the bed. I want to be potent
for her. At other times, I pleasure her with my dildo. I carefully
rub the jelly on its tip while she lies watching me, her breasts
spilling out of the negligee I have bought for her. I gently,
kindly, spread the cream on the tool of her pleasure. I feel I am
being kind to myself as I caress the false cock. No need to hide
the word any more. No need to hide my desires.

Let me be butch for you: I have been a femme for so long. I
know what your body is calling for. I know when I turn to you
before the sun has broken through the morning sky I will find
you wet and open, as if you had been waiting for a lover in a
dream. And so it is. When I turn you over in your sleep and
spread your legs, I feel your wetness before I enter you. Then
you begin to move in deep, deep circles, moving as in a dream
where bodies can swim through the air. I will move you from
your sleep up through waves of want. I will be deep inside of
you before the sun hits the building tops, and by the time it is
glinting off the water towers, I will have brought you to your
pleasure. Then I will give you back your sleep again.

I hear the old butches laughing. 'I was waiting for when
you would become Poppa,' Mabel said. 'It's about time,' she

chuckled. Then later in the day, for the first time in our thirty-five-year-old history, she called me Mr Nestle.

I look through the years and see the faces of women who have disappeared, women who tried to teach me the ways of our people. I am changing life now, but I travel with the old movements still inside me. She sometimes thrusts her long fingers into me as I lie on top of her and asks me to move on her, to rock on her fingers, but I fight the tempest in my own hips. I have bucked for many years. I have swirled my hips, I have thrust against women mountains, and I have moved them, but now I do not want my own movement to change the world. I want hers – her hips to call forth the new order, her surging hips that threaten to throw me off as she takes and mounts her pleasure.

Reach my love for all my hands can give, and I will give you more. Reach for all of us who began in our desire to grip the world between our legs, and reach now for me who has changed her form. I hear my elders, scarred and knowing, laughing kindly, saying to me, Come on girl. We welcome you.

A Different Place

Jay lay back in the tub, the hot water soaking her tired muscles. It had been a long day on the job, a day that seemed to consist of moving a hundred two-by-fours made of steel. She smiled, proud of what her forty-five-year-old body could still do. She discovered more and more of its strengths every day. Already her forearms were solid and her back was hard and broad. She loved construction work, loved to see the houses change shape under the guidance of her hands, loved to solve a problem of angles first with her mind and then with her tools. But she was still glad when quitting time came, particularly today. Her girl-friend from New York was spending the night, was, in fact, waiting for her in the bedroom.

She spread her legs, letting the hot water push against her, watched it circle her breasts – all breasts and muscle, she grinned. Not a bad combination. She was going to use both of them tonight. She knew what her honey wanted and was more than willing to comply. In fact, she had a few new ideas. She let her head drop back against the tub's edge. Sometimes it was wonderful being butch, to know clearly what your women lovers had been saying to you over the years, to know what brought on the wetness and how to slip your hand under them so they began moving. Not that it was rote by now: every time was different, at least in the beginning.

'Would you like your back washed?'

She looked up in surprise. Carol stood in the doorway,

dressed in a black slip, purple stockings, and lavender sling-back heels. The slip with its thin straps cupped her breasts, the lace resting on their fullness. The half-hard nipples pushed against the silk, while the rest of the slip showed the fullness of the body underneath. Carol was a big woman, and at this moment her flesh was proud.

'No, that's OK, I'll be out in a minute.'

They had only a short time together, and they both had already discovered that the best way of talking for them was making love. She laughed to herself. She knew a wanting femme when she saw one, but she also saw the love in Carol's eyes. Their love-making was not a test to see whether she could live up to her butch reputation. They knew months ago that they pleased each other that way. What she saw in Carol's eyes was desire, deep and stark, the sexual needing of an open woman. Carol wanted her, her hands, her arms, her breasts, her cunt, her tongue. This, Carol had made clear. She remembered the first time she had lifted Carol's legs back onto her chest, opening her up completely and then laying over her so she could feel Carol's wetness and the fullness of her clit under her. She did not need Carol to tell her that something special had happened that night, that cherishing and celebration had moved with them on that bed.

She slowly raised herself out of the tub, her tall body emerging from the heat. Sometimes life was hard, sometimes the loneliness and disappointments bore down on her like a lead sky, but tonight she felt good. She slowly dried herself and then sat on the closed toilet seat, taking long hauls of the joint she always treated herself to after a hard day. She knew Carol did not mind waiting, that expectation was a wonderful sharpener of desire. She had one more thing to do in preparation for the night. She ran her nails over her lips, checking for ragged edges. Then she carefully clipped any offending corners. She was taking responsibility for at least that part of the evening. Long ago she had learned that lovemaking was a combination of knowing the body's angles and curves and of pushing at its boundaries. Finally ready, she stood up, put a comb through her hair, and strolled into the bedroom. She paused in the doorway and just stood looking at the black-slipped woman who was lying on her stomach in the middle of the large bed. Her hips were moving slightly, and the slip had pulled up, exposing her full thighs above the purple stockings.

'How's my New York slut doing?' she said, in a low voice, as she circled the bed.

'Have you finished with all your preparations?' Carol answered, turning her head into the pillows. Then softly, 'I want you.'

'I know, baby, but I need just to watch you a little. I am going to sit in this chair and watch you grind your hips into that bed. I want to watch you move.'

Dusk fell into the room. The only sounds were the rustling of the slip and Jay's breathing. Then Carol started making little moaning sounds. Soon the words, 'Please, please don't make me wait any longer,' were heard. Jay quickly got up and lowered herself onto Carol's back. Her long broad body completely covered the woman beneath her. She secured Carol's hands above her head with her own, and just using the strength of her body and mouth, she started to take the woman beneath her. She bit into Carol's neck and cheek. She thrust her tongue into Carol's ear. And all the time Carol never stopped moving below her. She rode with her, her own wetness seeping onto Carol's legs, onto the slip. She put her hand between Carol's legs, running her fingers from the woman's cunt to her more protected place of entry. She felt Carol's body strain under her, almost lifting them both up as she tried to give Jay more room for touching.

'Tonight I am going to fuck you in a different place,' she whispered into Carol's ear, 'but you have to want it.' She brought her wet fingers back to Carol's asshole and pushed at its surface. Carol's body stiffened under her while at the same time Carol thrust herself back on Jay's finger.

'You tell me when you're ready. You let me know when you can take it.' She kept rubbing the soft skin, slipping in just the tip of her finger. Carol first moved her hips away and then slowly brought them back as if to test the promise of this new intrusion. Jay's own wetness shone on Carol's ass and she swelled with the knowledge of the entry to come.

'Give me your ass to tell me you are ready,' she said gently, her head above Carol's turned face. There was a pause, a silence in the room, and then the sound of a deep intake of breath as Carol slid her hips back onto Jay's hand. The sign had been given.

Jay positioned herself carefully over the woman's back, her arm drew back and the muscles that had lifted beams now poised for a more delicate power. She pushed her finger, blunt and strong, into Carol, feeling the tight resistance of the ass muscles, the strong sentinels protecting the soft world inside. Carol moaned, a different sound from when Jay penetrated her cunt. This was deeper, almost as if the body was finding a new voice for this more guarded entry.

'Yes baby, here.' She pushed harder. Carol was helping now by moving her ass back and forth, her whole back coming up under Jay's body, her arms stretching out above her head. Then Jay's finger was through – a wonderful mixture of tightness and tenderness grasped her. She moved in and out, penetrating a little more with each stroke. Carol's moans became louder. She tossed her head wildly, pushing the pillows up against the wall. Her whole body was pointed at Carol's finger, and now femme hunger was in control. Carol's full free body rocked under Jay, until suddenly, Carol raised herself up to her knees, forcing Jay back. Now it was clear that Carol wanted it all. She was thrusting her ass back and forth onto Jay's finger with her own rhythm, her breasts hanging full and dancing with each surge backward.

Jay looked down, watching and wondering at the strength of a woman's want. With her free hand she reached under Carol and opened her cunt lips. Wetness dripped down onto the sheets. Carol was rocking quietly now, all hips and ass, and the joy flowed through Jay's fingers, her arms. She had brought this woman to her pleasure, and she was going to bring her home. Everything became quiet. Only the sound of movement could be heard, and then Jay felt all of Carol tighten around her finger. 'Oh God,' the woman said, and fell forward, pulling Jay with her.

'Baby, so good, so good.'

Slowly, carefully, Jay moved out, stopping to let Carol rest as her ass muscles first fought release and then let her go with all her power. She fell over Carol, and they both lay that way for many minutes. Carol at first was still moving as if a phantom finger was inside of her. Jay could feel her ass muscles clench and grow loose over and over again. She heard her own breathing come back to normal and became aware of the longing in her own body. She liked the sweat that trickled between them, the river of their desire, liked the feeling of her breasts and muscles on this woman who had made a home for her in her body. She liked the smell in the room. Someday she would offer her own ass, but for now, she rested and loved.

The Three

The two femmes were large and loud and loving; the butch was lean and quiet and caring. On a hot August day, they met at the information booth at Penn Station and rushed together to make the early train to Sayville, Long Island. The butch sat in the middle, her white shirt setting off her slender but muscular arms. The three laughed and talked while sitting low in the old, stained train seats. Every once in awhile, the two femmes made allusions as to how they would pleasure their butch companion. From time to time, the older femme, a woman in her mid-forties, would run her hand along the butch's inner thighs. She knew the coming day would be complicated for her, but she felt perfectly secure in what her hands and mouth could do. She felt only love and caring for her two friends, the butch whom she had served several times before and who had always treated her with courtly concern, and the young vivacious femme whose flashes of beauty delighted her. The older woman knew she would watch over her young friend today, making sure that desire did not become loneliness.

Their train began to fill up with other gay women and men, all making the trek out to the Grove on New York's fabled Fire Island. After an hour's ride, they finally piled out of the train and into the waiting taxis driven by crusty old straight men that would take them to the patient ferries that had spent years carrying queens and bulldykes over the one deep channel in the Great South Bay.

The sun shone hot and clear, and the air was fresh with salt. They stood on line, taking turns getting coffee for each other, teasing each other, always the femmes' flamboyant spirits playing off of the butch's self-restraint. A bond was growing between them – three bodies, three histories open to the sun. After a short wait, the large white ferry welcomed them on and they settled themselves near the windows. The old boat pulled slowly out of its moorings and carefully maneuvered through the small channel that led to the wider bay. They sat closer together as the boat, now free of its restraints, surged forward, sending up banners of spray. In half an hour they reached the grey-planked pier and quickly walked the narrow boards that paved the streets of this gay village.

They spread their blankets close to the water. The butch stripped. She would wear nothing for the whole day. The two femmes wore one-piece bathing suits that presented their breasts well. They followed the butch as she walked into the water, her chiseled body entering the sea without a halt, while they flirted with the small waves and slowly let the coldness take them. Beyond the breakers, the three swam into each other's bodies in odd patterns, entwining their arms and legs around each other as the larger waves surged toward them. They held each other high up in the buoyant water. Once, the butch swam behind the older woman and cupped her breasts while the rest of her floated down into the sea.

Back on the blanket, the butch lay between them, and each femme would suck a nipple when the desire took her. They moved their hands down the resting butch's flanks soothing her, teasing her. The young femme took joy in running her long red nails down the butch's back, and they both watched as the butch pushed her body into the sand, her fingers and toes curling with pleasure. The older woman had made sandwiches for them all, and late in the afternoon she served them. How good it tasted – the warm summer tomatoes and sun-melted cheese on the grainy fresh bread, the ice water, the juicy peaches. Breasts and food, largeness and comfort, the sun, the sea, the wonder of freedom and the pleasure of kindness.

Toward evening, they changed their clothes, went to dinner, and danced a little. Then they separated for a while; the older woman, tired, sat on the wooden steps overlooking the quieted sea while the others went to visit friends and drink champagne.

They were reunited late in the evening in the small cottage where they would spend the night. The bed was large and low to the ground. The older woman, still fully clothed, sat with her head resting against the wall watching the butch give the younger femme a good hard fucking with her fingers. The butch kneeled over the woman who threw her hips back and forth as the hand demanded more and more from her. Her hips reached for the butch's arm. 'More, please give me more,' she moaned. The older woman felt nothing but appreciated the shapes and movement before her. She respected the intensity of pleasure-giving that held the butch taut and totally focused on the woman beneath her. The young femme reached out her hand to the older woman, wanting to draw her in. Finally, as if reaching down from a huge height, the older woman leaned forward and wrapped her fingers around the younger woman's full hair and held the woman's head in a slightly turned position. She stared down at the woman's beautiful face, knowing that the young femme enjoyed the restraint and the knowledge that her passion was being fully observed. 'Yes,' she said to the straining woman, 'take it all. All. This is what you've wanted for a long time, now take it all.' For a long while this fucking went on and then the two rested. The butch sat back on her heels. Both of them looked at the older woman. 'There is one among us who is fully clothed,' she said. Slowly the older woman relented. She leaned forward and removed her blouse so her full breasts hung free. She leaned back and raised her hips to remove her panties.

As if she was awakening from a long cold winter, she felt a desire growing in her. 'Fuck me with your cock,' she said in a low voice to the butch. The butch said, 'Yes, I would like to do that very much, yes.' The butch rose above the other two women and fastened on her leather harness, the black straps fitting smoothly over her taut belly and cheeks. She kneeled there with her cock jutting out, and the older woman rose to her, taking the cock between her nipple-hardened breasts. Then, with a smile, she pushed the butch back on the pillows and took her cock into her mouth. She licked it, swallowed it, squeezed it, and told the butch what a wonderful cock she had and how much she wanted it. Then, sensing the impatience of the younger femme, she moved aside so the other woman could also slide her lips down the wetted cock.

The butch moaned and moved her hips. 'Oh you girls, so good, so good.' The older woman lay down flat on the bed, and the younger femme let the cock slip out of her mouth. The butch moved to the foot of the bed and spread the legs of the older woman. First she reached for her cunt, and finding the moisture that she wanted, she positioned herself over the older woman. Then, slowly and exactly, she pushed her cock into her. The older woman felt the huge hunger come into her, and she raised her legs high up into the air. She started to move, rocking under the entering butch. Her hands found the muscled back, and her nails made their mark. 'Oh, I love to fuck you,' moaned the butch. She wrapped her legs tight around the butch's back, her heels pushing into the leathered cheeks so each thrust was deeper. Together they moved for long moments. Then slowly the older woman thought of her younger friend and started to take leave of her desire. 'I know she wants this too, I have had enough for now.' The butch withdrew and rested while the older woman worked a rubber over the wet cock. The younger woman was already lying down. She smiled gratefully at her older friend. The butch moved over, and once again she began to fuck. The older woman continued lying beside them both, with her eyes closed, hearing their moans and feeling the bed move with their rhythms.

At some point she was aware that the room had grown still. 'Are you all right?' a voice asked her. 'Yes,' she said. Then she said, 'I have a desire. Please someone touch me with their fingers.' She said this in a small voice, but a voice deep with the knowledge of her need. 'Of course,' her friends said. The butch moved to her right, and the femme moved to her left. She kept her eyes closed and put her hands on the two backs curving over her like protecting trees. She felt their mouths on her nipples. Then a wonder grew in her. Both of their hands were on her; together their fingers entered her. She could not tell whose hand was where until she felt the younger femme's nail flick over her wetness, and then, once again, both hands joined inside of her. 'Come to us, let it happen,' they whispered, and their loving fingers moved deeper into her, deeper than the cock they reached, and other fingers stroked her, caring fingers that knew her cunt's hardness, and slowly on their words and on their strokes, on their love and on their kindness, a fullness grew. 'Come to us now, let it go,' and with a heave of her hips that lifted them all, she did and did and did, throbbing around their joined fingers.

They slept wrapped around each other and woke early, drinking hot coffee on the edge of the dock, watching the sun come up. They sat in the drying wetness made by the spray from the early morning ferry, talking quietly about what they had given each other and what they had feared and what they had found. Then, tired, they made the trek home, sitting low in the old train seats, sharing whatever food they had left from the sun-drenched day on the beach.

My History With Censorship

My deep despair at the new antipornography movement and the censorial atmosphere that is fed by it is the legacy of my history. I came of age in a time that has marked me for life, the McCarthy period, the America of the 1950s. I entered the decade a lonely ten-year old living with an aunt and uncle because my mother could no longer afford to keep me. By the end of the fifties and early sixties, I was a practicing Lesbian, a member of CORE and SANE Nuclear Policy, a veteran of Freedom Rides and Woolworth picket lines, of voter registration drives and the march from Selma to Montgomery. I had refused to take cover in air raid drills and was on file as a subversive on my college campus.

I was a member of a group of students who protested against the House Un-American Activities Committee. We sat in disbelief as lawyers for the Committee screamed at and badgered an exhausted JoAnn Grant and Paul Robeson, Jr. I remember to this day the chair's words as we applauded every time one of them took the Fifth Amendment to protest the Committee's right to invade their privacy. He said, 'You people' – gesturing at us – 'are the scum of the earth.' I remember, as we huddled in the corridor during the break, a member of the Committee steering his girlfriend away from us, even brushing her dress aside to make sure it did not touch me. I remember the fifties in tones and gestures, in cadences of accusation. I will never forget the words, 'Are you now or have you ever been . . .' nor the frightened or tired or courageous eyes of those who had to hear them. I watched JoAnn Grant sit solidly while a lawyer for HUAC waved a piece of paper over her head, shouting, 'Did you ever attend a Pete Seeger concert?' She refused to answer. Any answer delivered her into the hands of those who had already condemned her.

I could go on and on about what it was like to get terrified students and teachers to sign petitions, what it was like to watch the hearings day after day on television, to watch Joseph McCarthy accuse, condemn, and try his victims all at the same time – but not by law. He always said, 'We do not send anyone to prison. We are not a court of law,' and yet, right before one's eyes and in one's neighbourhoods and over the radio, imagination and discussion were struck down.

Any dissension became a heroic act. If you spoke the wrong words or supported the wrong people, you were labeled un-American. You were sent into national, and in many cases private, exile. I watched people in their forties and fifties who had been labor organizers and social activists shrink from their children, withdraw into long, slow deaths. I heard the names read over the radio of those who were to be called in front of the Committee before the Committee even reached a city. Long enough in advance for employers to fire the accused, long enough to give neighbors the time to ostracize the marked family, long enough to give the stigmatized individual time to take his or her own life. None of this was done by legal power. It was done by the power of orthodoxy, of one prevailing view of how to make the country safe. It was not trial in a court of law with a jury; it was conviction by innuendo, by association, by labeling.

This is my historical and emotional starting point on the issue of censorship. These were the years I learned about censorship, the overt kind and the more subtle kind; the years I learned about a mentality that reserves for itself the words that mean everything good, and labels dissenters with any term that will send off the alarm. These were the years I learned about anonymous telephone calls warning people about the undesirables among them; the years I learned about visits to places of employment to make sure employers knew who they had working for them. It was the time I learned about silence, enforced by the fear of losing whole communities, about words and pictures never born because difference was a curse.

But all along I had another world to sustain me, the deviant criminalized world of butch-femme Lesbians in Village bars. Here, also, my behavior was policed. Here, also, I was part of a judged community. We were moral dangers. Here I learned that vice squads existed to keep obscenities like myself from polluting the rest of society. Here I learned how to take brutal insults to personal dignity and keep wanting and loving. Here I learned first what a community of women could do even when we were called the scum of the earth.

I worked in the gay liberation movement and the Lesbian liberation movement and then the women's movement for many years before I thought I could begin to explore the meaning of my own life, before in my own mind I was sure that we had won enough ground that I could raise some visions of resistance, other than the prevailing ones of the seventies. In 1981, I wrote an article called 'Butch-Femme Relationships: Sexual Courage in the 1950s' (see p. 89) and published a short story called 'Esther's Story' (see p. 28). That year marked for me the second McCarthy period in my life. Only this time, many of the holders of truth were women.

They called the organizers of conferences where I was speaking and told them I was a 'sexual deviant', labeling me as a dangerous person who betrays the feminist cause. The place where I earn my living, Queens College, was visited by a member of Women Against Pornography who saw it as her duty to warn a group of students and professors about me. 'Don't you know she is a Lesbian? Don't you know she practices S&M? Don't you know she engages in unequal patriarchal power sex?' (Butch and femme is what is meant here, I think.) I was told this when I was called to the Women's Center on campus and asked by the group of women students gathered there whether the accusations were correct. Only those of you who remember the cadence of those McCarthy words – 'Are you now or have you ever been . . .' – can know the rage that grew in me at this moment. These young women, so earnest in their feminism, were so set up for this sad moment. 'I cannot answer you,' I said, 'because to do so would bring back a world I have worked my whole life to see never come again.'

In the same year, I had another painful encounter with censorship that made me feel again the wounds of the past. One of the most terrible things about the McCarthy period was that friends or supporters could be severely punished for association with a 'known subversive'. In 1981, Susan Cavin of *Big Apple Dyke News* accepted my short story about a one-night stand with a passing woman for publication. On a May afternoon she called to tell me that the story had been called pornographic by a woman typesetter. She had received the following letter from the Addison Press management:

Dear Susan,
    I have just come from a meeting with the brass of this press regarding your paper. It seems that the typesetter that set the current issue of *B.A.D. News* made such a stink about 'offensive' material, that it has caused Mr Mills, the publisher, to reconsider our business relationship. Fearing legal problems by her potentially quitting over the issue, he would like me to communicate the following to your organization:

The Addison Press will decline to print any subsequent issues of *B.A.D. News* which contains explicit sex. This is primarily in reference to 'Esther's Story' and certain dream material . . .

The choice Susan had was to drop my story and keep their printer, or to drop the printer and keep 'Esther's Story'. I heard her voice telling me her predicament, and it all came back. *B.A.D.* did not have and does not have many resources to rely on for cushioning. My vision had gotten them into trouble. The paper was being punished for association with my ideas. Susan held the line and found a printer in New York who did not care what the words in the story said.

After the Barnard Conference on Sexuality in 1982, when *off our backs* was doing its reporting, I received a late-night call asking me if I had ever spoken out in favour of S&M relationships. That voice over the phone, my tiredness, the power on the other end, all brought home again the litany of the fifties. I had been told by a member of WAP that if I write about butch-femme relationships in the past, I am OK, but if I am writing about them now in any positive way, I am on the 'enemy list'. The labels chosen for me this time around are 'reactionary', 'heterosexually-identified Lesbian', 'believer in patriarchal sex'.

I now had a sense of what I faced – the Lesbian-feminist antipornography movement on one side, and the homophobia and antisex mentality of some straight people on the other.

Recently, sexually controversial writers lost another piece of ground. Amy Hoffman and I were asked to submit poetry to the *Women's Review of Books,* which is partially funded by Wellesley College. Both of us – she formally, me through a personal letter from a dissenting editor – were told that because our poetry was sexually explicit, the *Review* could not risk publishing it without endangering its funding from the college. Here is an example of censorship coming from a different direction: women's institutions that have some power but are afraid of using it.

Another way censorship works in our community, and it is very effective, is through the closing of bookstore doors to the works of stigmatized writers or publications judged offensive by 'feminist' standards, even when they are the creations of other feminists. For instance, two journals I write for, *Bad Attitude* and *On Our Backs,* have not been allowed into many women's bookstores around this country and in Canada because the contents were found to be 'prosadomasochistic, antifeminist, antiwoman, anti-Semitic, and racist'. Now, as you all know, these are the words that call for exile from our community, for there is no argument possible when this code is used. (As a Jewish woman, I find it ironic that Gentiles are in such a hurry to protect me from myself). The territory I am allowed had shrunk even more. Once you close the bookstores to a writer who has chosen to write for her community publications, you make the creation of an audience almost impossible.

Sadly, as a community, we have been inventive in discovering ways to control ideas. The refusal to allow someone to speak on a panel because she represents a certain point of view, the spreading of rumors about a woman's sexual practices, the refusal of meeting places to those who embarrass us, or the little white cards that popped up for a while in feminist bookstores, warning the potential reader of what to expect from a book, to protect the customer's sensibilities.

The latest accusation of pornography came my way last month. Now it is not my words, but a photograph of a part of my body and a dildo and a former lover's hand that has been called unacceptable. Here it is – a forty-five-year-old Lesbian's vagina being touched and opened by her lover's hand to insert a latex dildo. This photo is one of a series of my lover and me making love that appeared in *On Our Backs*. In a subsequent issue of *off our backs*, this photo and the magazine were called pornographic. If the ordinances that are being proposed were now in power, other Lesbians could get this journal banned from the stands, and this photograph would never be seen. But you see, this image is what my life has been about. This image is what the police tried to bash out of me. This image is what I was always told to keep secret. This image puts me and my body beyond the pale.

Think of what is happening. Think of the times and the traditional relationship between the state and sexual minorities. Think of the tools of repression some are helping to put in place.

The antipornography movement is helping to create a new McCarthy period in the Lesbian community. Some Lesbians are more acceptable than others. Leather and butch and femme Lesbians, transsexuals, Lesbian prostitutes and sex workers, writers of explicit sexual stories – little by little we are being rounded up. First we are distanced and told we are not feminists, even though many of us have spent years building the Movement. Then we are told that we are patriarchal, that we are the voices of submission and dominance, that we are heterosexual lesbians. The doors close to us. Then in a Reagan America, in a Jerry Falwell America, in a family-god-nation America, there will be nothing between us and the government the antiporn movement is helping to empower. Some Lesbian-feminists will turn us in and feel they have made the world safer for women by doing so.

All I have are my words and my body, and I will use them to say and picture the truths I know. I have been homeless before and I can be homeless again, but I almost think I have lived too long when I see Lesbians become members of the new vice squad.

Lesbian Memories 3:
A Night With Emma, 1986

The day was spent with Naomi and a group of gay men and women in Cold Springs, New York, which lived up to its name, but not cold really – damp and dripping, all fog and melting snow – a wonderful home with a fireplace and slippery walks into the forest, miniature waterfalls and a mist-shrouded lake, everything dripping.

Then home to Jones Street, tired, walking up the steps to Emma's apartment. The door opened and there she stood. White T-shirt with the sleeves rolled up, 501 jeans, head cocked to one side. 'Where the hell have you been?' Behind her shone the candlelight. I paused, tired and middle-aged, and took in the sight – her beautiful face, her small tight body, her rowdy stance, and I loved the courage of her demand. Quickly I changed, and with her beer can in one hand and me in the other, we set out for the Gay Film Festival.

She stood on line behind me, her arms around my breasts. I understood, then, the women in their mid-forties who seek out affairs with young men; I understood the wonderful mixture of ages and bodies, the promises of different things we told each other with each touch. She could have been my daughter, my son, but she was my lover. In the theater, surrounded by the other Lesbians, she leaned over me and whispered, 'I am going to fuck you on my couch or on your living room floor tonight before you take a bath. The choice is yours.' I laughed, amazed at her audacity. She knew I had a need to bathe before love-making, a fear that my body, sweating in the day world, could not stand the glare of intimacy, that I was not clean enough to be touched without the cleansing water. But she was demanding spontaneous lust, and she got it.

She marched me home after the film, through the streets I had haunted in my early queer days, now the streets of my lover's home. I felt the drive in her, her refusal to accept old ways, and I knew I would feel her hands in me before I felt the water.

Play My Darling, Play

The sun came up hot and sharp over the Truro hills and the two middle-aged women were up early to greet it. 'Let's do it today,' the blonde one said to the dark one. After a quick breakfast, they donned their riding gear: shorts, T-shirts that pictured big women holding their bikes up to the sky, gloves cut off at the knuckles, sweatshirts wrapped around their shoulders. Outside of their rented cottage, they stood for a moment breathing in the pine air, feeling their bodies relax into the day. Their steeds were resting against the side wall of their two-week home, the sun already glinting off the handle bars. 'Come on girl.' Now it was time to put on the helmets, the white domes striped with red signaling this was to be a mighty day. Water bottles were attached to the side bars, small tools were stored in the little black bags that rode under the seats.

The tires crunched as the two women mounted and moved slowly over the mixture of broken shells and sand that was their driveway. Highway 6 was still quiet, but the morning air was alive with summer life. The seagulls swooped overhead, making their way to the ocean that lay just behind the cliffs; the beach roses, clinging to the grey weathered fences, embraced the new day with open petals and crisp pink colors. The wind was a rider's friend, just strong enough to cool their shoulders. No longer young, not often free, the two women slowly built up speed. Soon they found the abandoned railroad bed that had been turned into a twenty-six mile pathway for adventurers such as themselves. For as long as they could go, the two would travel through the salt ponds and scrub pine forests, through flower-sprinkled meadows and past an old harbor that carried the memory of New England whaling boats and seamen's courage. Their city muscles would find new strength. Each mile, each deep breath, would open another tired place, and though their bodies would work hard and long, their spirits would soar into the sun.

Margaret

1.

'What will you do when your cunt, dripping wet, cries out for my fingers?'

I moan, entered by her words, my head falling hard onto her breasts. We are engaged in a battle of frustration, as she will later call it. We fight each other, both with our bodies and our words, fight the need we have and the restrictions we have placed on our relationship. I am on top of her, my black slip shoved up over my ass, my body using all its strength to pin her under me. I taunt her. 'What kind of wimpy-assed butch are you?'

'Butch enough to make you cry out when you come.'

I suck her nipple into my mouth, pressing it hard against my palate. She breathes in sharply, as she always does when her nipples become mine. When she is on her back, her body's fullness begs for touch. When she is above me, her muscled back, her wide shoulders, her powerful forearms present a different kind of woman, but always the softness of her breasts precedes her. And then she is on me, fully, biting my neck, forcing my thighs apart. I want to scream words I have never said before to her; I want to be all breasts and ass for her. She lives her desire as no woman I have ever known. She trembles with it, pushes against it, breathes it in with huge moans. I bend my leg so she can ride my thigh. I feel her wetness on me as she pushes, pushes, her head buried in my neck. Her fingers welcome the hardness of my nipples. My breasts, already large, swell to her taking. I thrust up against her.

The first time we were ever together, on a warm summer night in Michigan surrounded by hundreds of new-time Lesbians, this young woman came on me in the old butch way – on top of me, moving on my leg. My body and her dreams driving out her roar of pleasure.

Now, a year later, my leg trembles under the power of her concentrated movement, and then her whole body becomes a single wave. She comes heaving against my leg, collapsing onto me. I hold her, so dear, waiting for the pounding of her heart to quiet. I had thought this gift of a woman coming on top of me had fled the world, but Margaret, who wears feathers and dreams of goddesses, carries the old ways of women loving deep within her.

2.

She sat naked on the couch, her legs spread out, her fingers moving rapidly over her clit. The unicorn tattooed on her thigh trembled with the tension of her body, but it was clear to me that she needed something else. I positioned myself on the floor in front of her, lifting up my nightgown as I knelt, my head cushioned on my crossed arms, my large ass touching her knee. She groaned, 'Yes, baby, that's good,' and for a time all I heard was the winglike movement of her fingers on herself. I kept my position, thinking how smart I was to know what would help her. Then she leaned over and began to squeeze my ass over and over again, until finally she slipped two fingers into me. Now she rocked us both with her own movement for pleasure. I fell lower onto the floor while my ass reached for her even more, and then with the wonderful roar I have come to know, she came. Before I thought it was possible, without resting, she fell on me, and only then did I become aware of the cold tiles beneath my breasts. All my calculated moves fled as she moved me on that floor. The rest of the night was in her hands.

Lesbians And Prostitutes:
An Historical Sisterhood

The prevalence of lesbianism in brothels throughout the world has convinced me that prostitution, as a behavior deviation, attracts to a large extent women who have a very strong latent homosexual component. Through prostitution these women eventually overcome their homosexual repression.

> Frank Caprio, *Female Homosexuality:*
> *A Psychodynamic Study of Lesbianism* (1954)

'We're having the meeting during Lesbian/Gay Freedom Week because many prostitute women are Lesbians – yet we have a fight to be visible in the women's and the gay movements. This is partly due to our illegality but also because being out about our profession, we face attitudes that suggest we're either a 'traitor to the women's cause' or not 'a real Lesbian'.

> Speaker at 'Prostitutes:
> Our Life – Lesbian and Straight',
> San Francisco, June 1982

These indoor prostitutes are on the rise. Captain Jerome Piazza of the Manhattan South Public Morals Division estimates that there are at least 10,000 inside 'pros' in the city. Women Against Pornography contends that there are

25,000 prostitutes working inside and outside the city, over 9500 of them on the West Side alone.

West Side Spirit, June 17, 1985

To prepare for the United Nations' Conference on Women, the Kenyan government put new benches in the parks, filled in the potholes and swept the prostitutes off the streets.

New York Times, July 15, 1985

The original impulse behind this essay was to show how Lesbians and prostitutes have always been connected, not just in the male imagination but in their actual histories. I hoped that by putting out the bits and pieces of this shared territory I would have some impact on the contemporary feminist position on prostitution as expressed by the feminist antipornography movement. But in doing my reading and listening, a larger vision formed in me: the desire to give back to working women their own history, much as we have been trying to do in the grassroots Lesbian and gay history projects around the country. Whores, like queers, are a society's dirty joke. To even suggest that they have a history, not as a map of pathology but as a record of a people, is to challenge sacrosanct boundaries. As I read of the complicated history of whores, I realized once again I was also reading women's history with all its contradictions of oppression and resistance, of sisterhood and betrayal. In this work I will try to honor both histories – that of the woman whore and the woman queer.

First, my own starting point. In the bars of the late fifties and early sixties where I learned my Lesbian ways, whores were part of our world. We sat on barstools next to each other, we partied together, and we made love together. The vice squad, the forerunners of the Morals Division with whom Women Against Pornography have no qualms collaborating, controlled our world, and we knew clearly that whore and queer made little difference when a raid was on.

This shared territory broke apart, at least for me, when I

entered the world of Lesbian-feminism. Whores and women who looked like whores became the enemy, or at best, misguided oppressed women who needed our help. Some early conferences on radical feminism and prostitution were marked by the total absence of working women in any part of the proceedings. The prostitute was once again the other, much as she was earlier in the feminist purity movements of the late nineteenth century.

A much closer connection came home to me when I was reading through my mother's legacy, her scribbled writings, and discovered that at different times in her life my mother had turned tricks to pay her rent. I had known this all along in some other part of me, particularly when I had shared her bed in the Hotel Dixie in the heart of Forty-second Street during one of her out-of-work periods, but I had never let the truth of my mother's life sink in in many ways, and this was one of them.

And finally, in my own recent life I have entered the domain of public sex. I write sex stories for Lesbian magazines, I pose for explicit photographs for Lesbian photographers, I do readings of sexually graphic materials dressed in sexually revealing clothes, and I have taken money from women for sexual acts. I am, depending on who is the accuser, a pornographer, a queer, and a whore. Thus, both for political and personal reasons, it became clear to me that this writing had to be done.

One of the oldest specific references I found to the connection between Lesbians and prostitutes was in the early pages of William W. Sanger's *History of Prostitution* (1859). Similar to the process of reading early historical references to Lesbians, one must pry the women loose from the judgmental language they are embedded in. Prostitution, he tells us, 'stains the earliest mythological records',(2) He works his way through the Old Testament, revealing that Tamar, daughter of Judah, covered her face with her veil, the sign of a harlot. Many of the women 'driven to the highways for refuge, lived in booths and tents, where they combined the trade of a peddlar with the calling of a harlot'.(3–7) Two important themes are set out here, the wearing of clothes as both an announcement and an expression of stigma, and the issue of women's work.

It is in Sanger's chapter on ancient Greece that we find the first concrete reference to Lesbian history. Attached to the Athenian houses of prostitution called *dicteria* 'were schools where young women were initiated into the most disgusting practices by females who had themselves acquired them in the same manner'.(48) Here is evidence of intergenerational same-sex activity which is also used for the transmission of subculture survival skills. A more developed connection is revealed in his discussion of one of the four classes of Greek prostitutes – the flute players known as *Auletrides*. These gifted musicians were hired to play and dance at banquets, after which their sexual services could be bought. Once a year, these women gathered to honor Venus and to celebrate their calling. No men were allowed to attend these early rites, except through special dispensation.

> Their banquet lasted from dark till dawn with wines, perfumes, delicate foods, songs and music. Once a dispute broke out between two guests as to their respective beauty. A trial was demanded by the company and a long and graphic account is given of the exhibition [by the recording poet] but modern tastes will not allow us to transcribe the details . . . It has been suggested that these festivals were originated by, or gave rise to, those enormous aberrations of the Greek feminine mind known to the ancients as Lesbian love. There is grave reason to believe something of the kind. Indeed, Lucius affirms that while avarice prompted common pleasures, taste and feeling inclined the flute players toward their own sex. On such a repulsive theme it is necessary not to enlarge.(50)

Oh, how wrong the gentlemen scholar is. This passage, far removed from the original, may be a mixture of some Greek history and much Victorian attitude, but it is provocative both in its tidbit of information and the language it uses to express it.

In 1985 I attended my first Michigan Women's Music Festival. All during the festivities I kept thinking of those early flute players pleasuring each other, and I wondered if it would change some of the themes of cultural feminism if this historical legacy were recognized.

The primacy of dress codes runs throughout the history of prostitution. This drama of how prostitutes had to be socially marked to set them aside from the domesticated woman, and how the prostitute population responded to these demands of the state, led me to think many times of the ways in which Lesbians have used clothes to announce themselves as a different kind of woman. Prostitutes, even up to the turn of the century, were described as unnatural women, creatures who had no connection to wives and mothers, much as Lesbians were called, years later, a third sex. Citing an 1830 text, Ruth Rosen writes in *The Lost Sisterhood*, 'She [the prostitute] could serve men's needs because a great gulf separated her nature from that of other women. In the female character, there is no midway. It must exist in spotless innocence or hopeless vice.'(6) This view of the prostitute as another species of woman is to continue through the years. In 1954, Jess Stern, a popularizer of erotic subcultures, writes: 'The only thing I was sure about then was that the prostitute is no more like other women than a zebra is like a horse. She is a distinct breed, more different from her sisters under the skin than she – or the rest of society – could possibly realize . . . They have one common denominator, as essential quality that distinguishes them from other women – a profound contempt of the opposite sex.'(13,15) Both dykes and whores, it appears, have an historical heritage of redefining the concept of woman.

To make sure the prostitute did not pass into the population of 'true women', through the centuries different states set up regulations controlling her self-presentation and physical movements. In Classical Greek times, all whores had to wear flowered or striped robes. At some time, even though no law decreed it, the prostitutes dyed their hair blonde in a common gesture of solidarity. In the Roman period, 'the law prescribed with care the dress of prostitutes on the principle that they were to be distinguished in all things from honest women. Thus they were not allowed to wear the chaste *stola* which concealed the form or the *fillet* with which Roman women bound their hair or to wear shoes or jewels or purple robes. These were the insignia of virtue. Prostitutes wore the *toga* like men . . . Some even went one step further in a bold announcement of their trade and wore over the green toga a short white jacket, the badge of adultery'. (Sanger, 75) A provocative point made throughout the history of state regulations concerning prostitute dress is the inclusion of men's apparel as part of the stigmatizing process. For instance, in the late-fourteenth century, we are told by Lydia Otis, 'Prostitutes were required to carry a mark on their left arm . . . whereas in Castres (in 1375) the statutory sign was a man's hat and a scarlet belt.'(80) Here, as in Lesbian history, cross-dressing signals the breaking of women's traditional erotic, and therefore social, territory.

For the next three hundred years, prostitutes were marked by the state, both in being forced to wear a certain kind of clothes or identifying symbol – like a red shoulder knot, a white scarf, or, in a chilling prefiguring of mid-twentieth century history, a yellow cord on their sleeves – and by physical restrictions. As I read of the demanded dress codes, I was reminded of the warning older Lesbians gave me in the fifties as I prepared for a night out: always wear three pieces of women's clothing so the vice squad can't bust you for transvestism.

The states also drew up litanies of control defining the multitude of ways prostitutes could lose their social freedoms. In fifteenth-century France, a prostitute faced up to three months imprisonment if she was:

1 To appear in forbidden places
2 To appear at forbidden hours
3 To walk through the streets in daylight in such a way as to attract the notice of people passing. (Sanger, 150)

Five centuries later on another continent, the language of control has the same purpose but is more elaborate in its requirements, according to H.B. Woolston:

Rules for Reservation, El Paso, Texas, 1921

Women must:
1 Keep screen doors fastened on inside and keep curtain on lower half of screen door.
2 Sit back from doors and windows and not sit with legs crossed in a vulgar manner and must keep skirts down
3 Remain in rooms until after twelve o'clock, and when they come out on the street they must not be loud or boisterous or be playing with each other or with men. They must not be hugging men or women around the street or be trying to pull men into their cribs.

Women must not:
4 Sit in windows with screens down or stand in doors at any time.
5 Cross the street in middle of block, but must go to Second or Third Street and cross over.
6 Yell or scream from one room to the other or use loud, vulgar language.
7 Wear gaudy clothes or commit any act of flirtation or other act that will attract unusual attention on the streets.
8 Work with the lights out. (336–337)

I want to reproduce these decrees of control here because they are the prostitutes' historical documents of oppression. Few, I think, realize how completely the police could infringe on a working woman's life. They also foreshadow the control the vice squad was to have in Lesbian bars in the fifties, when even our bathroom habits were under surveillance.

Yet within these constraints, some women were able to turn their social prisons into social freedoms, becoming the intellectually free women of their day. The history of prostitution has its luminaries, women who used the power of their stig-matized place to become unusual women, women who lived outside the domestic restrictions that entrapped the vast majority of their sisters. Thus we have the biographies of famous courtesans, extolling their wit and depicting their involvement in literature and politics. Successful prostitution accomplished for some whores what passing for men did for some Lesbians: it gave them freedom from the rigidly controlled women's sphere.

A rich untapped source of Lesbian history is diaries and biographies of courtesans, madams, strippers, and other sex workers. Of course, to take these documents seriously, as seri-ously as the letters of female friends in the nineteenth century, is going to test the class and attitude boundaries of many fem-inist scholars. Another problem is that fact and fiction are often intertwined in these works, but both the fact and the more imaginative creations can be valuable sources in piecing together a fuller Lesbian history.

In Cora Pearl's *Grand Horizontal: The Erotic Memoirs of a Passionate Lady*, written in 1873, several mentions are made of female same-sex activities. The first takes place in a French convent school for poor girls in the year 1849. The narrator soon discovers that her schoolmates had learned to please each other. 'The degree of interest which my companions exhibited not only in their own but in each other's bodies was something strange to me.' The author then goes on to describe at length a sexual initiation scene in a bathtub under the careful tutelage of Liane, an older student who brings two of the younger girls to orgasm as the rest of the girls watch. At night, the courtesan-to-be says, 'I was taught the pleasures of the body which within a year or two became so keen that I was convinced that anyone who neglected them was a dunce indeed. These pleasures were exclusively female.' She carefully assures her reader that these pleasures were never forced on any girl too young or inexperienced to receive them, and then goes on to tell how she discovered that the older women, the school mistresses, also enjoyed Lesbian sex. 'Suddenly going into one of the classrooms to fetch a set of needles I discovered Bette on her knees before Sister Rose, one of the younger and prettier mistresses, her head thrust beneath her skirts. I had time to glimpse an expression on her face which was familiar to me as that on the faces of my friends at certain times of mutual pleasure.'(22)

The narrator develops a philosophy of pleasure based on these early sexual encounters, but female bonding is also a part of the experience. 'Our nightly experiments in the dormitory can be imagined. Eugenie, my particular friend hearing from Bette of the incident with Soeur Rose, determined to introduce me to the pleasure the lips and tongue can give, and I did not find that pleasure at all mitigated by distaste; then as since, I was keenly conscious that one of the greatest joys in life is experiencing the pleasure one can give to one's lovers. And now I was fully grown, and keen to experience myself the full extent of the pleasure I could give to others. For the most part we fell into pairs, and there grew up between many of us true and real devotion, unmatched since . . . Our experiments were by no means without their effect on my later career, for I learned at that time to be wary of no activity which pleasure was the result of.'(23)

Later on in the memoirs, Cora goes to bed with a Lesbian wife of a male client, a woman described in what we would call today butch terms. 'She then invited me to warm her which being a guest I did. She was of a sturdy and muscular build, with breasts which were firm rather than full, indeed no more presenting the chest of a woman than of some men I have known.' The wife asks Cora to share her bed, explaining, 'Not long after marriage she discovered that men and their figures were if not entirely repugnant at least unexciting to me, whereas her female admiration for the female figure was what she could not but give vent to.'(166) Cora muses as they make love, 'Another woman must more securely know through pleasuring herself how to give pleasure to a fellow of her sex.' In the world of women's history research, we often hear the statement, but 'nice' women did not talk about sex in those days. If we turn to different sources, however, like the writings and records of sexually defined women, we may discover that women of different social positions talked in all kinds of ways. The challenge is whether we really want to hear their voices and how we will fit them into what Adrienne Rich has called the Lesbian continuum.

In 1912, a Lesbian prostitute anarchist named Almeda Sperry enters both histories by writing a love letter to Emma Goldman that uses a frankness of language we hunger for in our research. 'Dearest, it is a good thing that I came away when I did – in fact, I would have had to come away anyway. If I had only had the courage enough to kill myself when you reached the climax then – then I would have known happiness for at that moment I had complete possession of you . . . Satisfied, ah God no. At this moment I am listening to the rhythm of the pulse coming in your throat. I am surging along with your lifeblood, coursing in the secret places of your body. I cannot escape the rhythmic spurt of your love juices.' (Falk, 174–5) Emma Goldman, we learn from Candace Falk's work, *Love, Anarchy and Emma Goldman*, was no stranger to frank depictions of desire, so it comes as no surprise that she inspired such a passionate response. Almeda Sperry, Lesbian and prostitute, should be as much a part of our history as Natalie Barney or the Ladies of Llangollen. But neither her language nor her profession is genteel. Although she may not fit easily into academic reading lists, the understanding of our history, of women's history, will be poorer for the exclusion of such voices.

In the memoirs of Nell Kimball, a heterosexual madam, many references are made to Lesbians. One of the more famous madams of her times was Emma Flegel, born in 1867, a Jewish immigrant from Lubeck, Germany, who came to America and worked as a cook's helper until circumstances forced her to marry and settle in St. Louis. There she opened a highly successful brothel and was known throughout the subculture for her love affairs with her girls. 'Emma apparently always had a favorite among her girls, with whom she'd carry on a crush for a year or so before seeking a new favorite' (information sent to Lesbian Herstory Archives). Here we see how ethnic Lesbian history can interconnect with the general story of both Lesbians and prostitutes, as long as shame does not get in the way. This does not mean a history without concepts or conflicts, but it does mean a commitment to opening up new territory, to the inclusion of women who may challenge prevailing Lesbian-feminist categories.

Besides recognizing the history of prostitutes as a valuable source for Lesbian history, another connection that emerges is the Lesbian customer and protector of prostitutes. In the wonderful and moving story of Jeanne Bonnet, a passing woman of San Francisco in the 1870s (given life by the work of the San Francisco Lesbian and Gay History Project and Alan Berube in particular), we meet a woman who first came to the Barbary Coast brothels as a customer but in 1876 decided to enlist some of the women she visited in her all women's gang. They ended their lives as prostitutes and survived by petty stealing. One of the women she won away from her pimp, Blanche Buneau, became her special friend. But the anger of the scorned man followed the two women into the privacy of their life. In the words of Alan Berube: 'After dark, according to Blanche, Jeanne sat in a chair smoking her pipe and drinking a glass of cognac. She took off her male attire, got into their bed, and with her head propped up on her elbow, waited for Blanche to join her. Blanche sat down on the edge of the bed and bent over to unlace her shoes when a shot was fired through the window hitting Jeanne, who cried, "I join my sister," and died.' We are told that her funeral in the year of 1876 in San Francisco was attended by 'many women of the wrong class . . . the tears washing little furrows through the paint on their cheeks'. (Berube, LHA)

In Jonathan Katz's *Gay/Lesbian Almanac: A New Documentary*, we find a mention of a 'female case, R., age thirty-eight', who 'proclaims her characteristics in the most flagrant way through her manner of dress which is always the most masculine, straight tailored hats and heavy shoes. She makes a living by prostituting herself homosexually to various

women.'(339) Here embedded in the language of Dr. Douglas
C. McMurtrie, author of 'Some Observations on the Psychology
of Sexual Inversion in Women', we have another clue to
Lesbian history. Perhaps R. will seem more worthy of our attention when we are told by the doctor: 'R. feels absolutely no
shame or delicacy regarding her position. In the city . . . she
frequents public places dressed in a manner to attract general
notice. She is heaped with contempt and scorn by the normal
and feminine women who see her. She seems, however, to
rather glory in this attention and adverse criticism.'(339)

Homosexual women visiting Lesbian prostitutes is also
documented by Frank Caprio, a pop psychologist from the
fifties, who captures that decade's combination of prejudice
and sensationalism perfectly. 'In these brothels, which are
referred to as Temples of Sappho, lesbian practices consist of
intercourse via the use of a penis substitute, mutual mastur-
bation, tribadism and cunnilingus. While many of the clients
are passively homosexual, they often assume an active role and
in this way they find an outlet for their repressed homosexual
cravings. One of these Temples of Sappho in Paris, catering to
women clients, is lavishly furnished. A bar occupies a portion
of the lower floor where alcoholic beverages may be obtained.
The lesbian inmates are attired in transparent, sex-appealing
undergarments, and stimulate their women clients with in-
viting gestures. Private rooms in an upper floor are devoted to
sexual liaisons which follow the preliminary acquaintanceship
. . .'(93)

It is the challenge of Lesbian historians to sort out what is
bona fide Lesbian culture here and what is Caprio's imagination, but we do know from oral histories that such places
existed – and not only in exotic Paris. Mabel Hampton, for
example, a Black eighty-four-year-old New York Lesbian, tells
about a brothel in Harlem during the thirties that catered
only to women customers, and whose Lesbian madam kept a
shotgun by the door to scare away curious men.

One important point I would like to make is the need to
include questions about prostitution and prostitutes in any oral

history done with older Lesbian women. If the message is given that this is shameful territory, that the 'feminist' interviewer would be appalled by femme whores or butch pimps, by a myriad of cultural and personal overlappings of these two worlds, this whole part of our women's history will again go underground. We will lose insight and understanding about how Lesbians in particular and women in general who live outside the pale of domestic arrangements organize their lives.

Lesbians have and still do turn to prostitutes for sexual comfort, as well as work as prostitutes themselves. In 1984 in a small town in Tennessee, the police set up an entrapment net using a policewoman posing as a prostitute. After the arrests for soliciting were made, the names of the arrested were published in the town's newspaper. In an article entitled, 'Police Sex Sting Nets 127,' we hear a woman's voice:

> . . . and many of them admitted they had made a mistake.
>
> 'Some mistakes you can only make one time,' said the only woman charged during the three-day undercover operation. 'My mother and grandmother are ministers in Missouri. I'm not a low-life.'
>
> The woman who turned 24 today, sat in her car and wept after being given her citation. She was convinced she would be fired from her job, which she only recently gained.
>
> 'I do have some girlfriends, but things aren't great right now,' she told the police decoy.
>
> She later told a reporter that she thought the undercover operation was unfair.
>
> 'I think the cops should have said, 'Hey, don't do it again,' and let me live my life.
>
> 'You're talking about a story. I'm talking about my career.'
> (*Tennessean*, November 22, 1984)

In the early decades of the twentieth century, Lesbians and prostitutes were often confused in the popular and legal imagination. Mabel Hampton, who lived as a Lesbian from her early teens on, tells how she was arrested in 1920 at a white woman's house while waiting for a friend. Because of an anonymous tip that a wild party was going on, 'three bulls' came crashing through the door: even though Ms Hampton clearly was a 'woman's woman', she was arrested for prostitution and sent to Bedford Hills Reformatory for two years at the age of nineteen. According to Ms Hampton, many of the girls arrested for prostitution were, in fact, Lesbians. Taking adversity as a challenge, Mabel Hampton sums up her Bedford Hills experience by commenting, 'I sure had a good time with all those girls.' Mabel's good time was not hers alone. Estelle Freedman has chronicled the scandal over Lesbianism that hit Bedford Hills a few years later. Here we have another clue to a fuller Lesbian history: we need to go back to prison records and start exploring the lives we will find summarized in the terse sentences of the state.

We know from *The Lost Sisterhood* that prostitutes had become the victims of antivice campaigns in the twenties, campaigns that established practices of harassment, surveillance, and arrest later to be used against clearly defined Lesbians and their gathering places. 'The growth of special courts, vice squads, social workers, and prisons to deal with prostitution'(19) became the Lesbian legacy of the forties and fifties.

H.B. Woolston details the methodology. A police form used in interrogating arrested prostitutes in the 1920s shows the following categories under the heading of general health: 'Use Liquor, Drugs, Perversion, Homosex.'(331) It is in this decade that police boast of the new methods they developed to humiliate working women: 'A spectacular method for striking terror into the heart of the wrongdoers is the sudden and sometimes violent raid. A patrol wagon dashes up to the suspected house. Police scramble out and attack various entrances and exits and round up the inmates.'(214)

Fifty years later, Barbara Turrill, a prostitute, describes a bar raid with these words: 'You can feel them in the air, when you're in the bar, and sometimes they take the whole bar out, all of the girls sitting at the bar, and put them in the wagon and take them downtown and put them through a lot of hassles.

They can just walk in and take you for I and D (idle and disorderly persons) if nothing else.'(8) Any Lesbian who has been in a bar raid would recognize this description.

Another striking example of how the two worlds come together is shown in an excerpt from an oral history by Rikki Streicher, owner of a Lesbian bar in San Francisco. The time is the forties, but the incident has its roots in the 1900s:

> I was working as a waitress at the Paper Doll. Somebody called up and said the cops were on the way. I sent everybody home and stayed. So I was the only one there, so they took me in. If you were a woman, their charges were usually 72 VD which meant they took you in for a VD test and 72 hours is how long it took for the test. They took me in but decided not to book me. So a friend came down and got me out.(5)

Here the Lesbian is being policed with a procedure growing out of the social attitude viewing the prostitute as a carrier of a social disease. In the medical records of the state, Lesbian and prostitute history often become one. According to Dr. Virginia Livingston, a staff physician of the Brooklyn Hospital for Infectious Disease during WW II, 'the hospital had a clinic for prostitutes and many of the prostitutes were Lesbians'. (WBAI interview, March 7, 1980) The connection between sex and disease which was to haunt prostitutes during the war years, causing many enforced incarcerations, is once again in the social air. And once again, whores and queers must be on the alert for the loss of civil liberties in the face of social panic.

Because prostitutes were the first policed community of outlaw women, they were forced to develop a subculture of survival and resistance. We have seen some details of this culture in the earlier discussion of clothes and women's gatherings. But to enter modern times, I suggest much unexplored Lesbian history lies in the so-called dens of legalized vice that sprang up in the first decade of the twentieth century. In the famous red light districts of that time, in New Orlean's

Storyville, in San Francisco's Barbary Coast, in New York's Five Points and Tenderloin districts, Lesbian stories are waiting to be told.

An ad from one of the famous blue books of the period included in its listings of sexual services available a reference to female homosexual entertainment. (Rosen, 82) From the prostitute subculture comes the phrase, 'in the life', the way Black Lesbians will define their Lesbian identities in the thirties and forties. From this world comes the use of a buzzer or light to signal the arrival of the police in the back room of a Lesbian bar, a tradition still strong in the Lesbian fifties. Rosen tells us that 'These districts although in a state of transition still offered women a certain amount of protection, support and human validation . . . The process of adapting to the district . . . involved a series of introductions to the new language . . . the humor and folklore of the subculture.'(102) A prostitute in Kate Millet's *The Prostitution Papers* will comment years later, 'It's funny that the expression *go straight* is the same expression for gay people. It's funny that both these worlds should use that expression.'(41)

The final and perhaps most ironic connection between these two worlds that I want to discuss is how Lesbians and prostitutes are tied together in the psychology literature. One of the prevailing models for explaining the 'sickness' of prostitutes in the fifties was that prostitutes were really Lesbians in disguise who suffered from an Oedipus complex and therefore were hostile to men. As Caprio put it in his 1954 work, 'While it seems paradoxical to think of . . . prostitutes having strong homosexual tendencies, psychoanalysts have demonstrated that prostitution represents a form of pseudoheterosexuality, a flight from homosexual repressions.'(93) Helen Deutsch saw the problem in another interesting light. Identification for the prostitute was with the masculine mother and she 'has the need to deride social institutions, law and morality as well as the men who impose such authority.' (Bullough, 89) Another type of prostitute, Deutsch continues, is 'the woman who renounces tenderness and feminine gratification in favor of the aggressive masculinity she imitated'.(89) thus making her a latent lesbian.

Mixed in with the attempts to explain the sickness of the prostitute are the stories of women's lives. Caprio, for example, says he had done hundreds of interviews with Lesbian prostitutes from around the world. I cannot bear to spend too many words on this connection because I have felt the weight of these theories in my own life. My mother took me to doctors in the early fifties to see who could cure her freak daughter. It is enough to say that prostitutes and Lesbians have a shared history of struggle with the law, religion, and medicine, all attempting to explain and control the 'pathology' of these unusual women. Lesbian prostitutes have suffered the totality of their two histories as deviant women – they have been called sinful, sick, unnatural, and a social pollution. In the decade of Lesbian-feminism, they have not been called anything because they are invisible. Even so astute and caring a gay historian as Jeffrey Weeks feels the need to deny their existence in the service of a patriarchally free Lesbian history. The existence of Lesbian prostitutes is not a blemish on the story of our people; their stories give us clues about the complexity of Lesbian history specifically, and about women's history in general.

While I was doing this research, I was struck by the connections between three seemingly disparate worlds: the Lesbian, the prostitute, and the nun – all examples of undomesticated women who form communities marked by women-bonding. In 1985, the Lesbian-feminist community enthusiastically welcomed the world of Lesbian nuns into the Lesbian continuum. And recent research done on prostitution in medieval society by Leah Lydia Otis bears out a profound connection between at least two of these groups. In the fifteenth century, it was not unusual for whole houses of prostitutes, run by women, to turn themselves into a convent when they reached the age of retirement. Thus the sisterhood was preserved and the women could continue to live in one version of medieval separatism. As always, the same-sex documentation is harder to find, but we do have a glimmer. 'In Grasse in 1487 a prostitute was sentenced to pay a 50s fine for having disobeyed the vicar's regulation forbidding prostitutes to dance with honest women.'(81)

Four centuries later, prostitutes and nuns are joined once again by a historical tragedy that called forth the highest acts of human courage. Vera Lasker in her passionate work, *Women in the Resistance and in the Holocaust: The Voice of Eye-witnesses*, tells us that 'some of the best safe houses for resistance fighters were brothels and convents'.(6) She also asserts that some of the most daring women in the service of the resistance were prostitutes.(7) The full story of the fate of prostitutes both in the resistance movement and in the concentration camps still has to be told, and I hope the one who does it is a whore. I am sure that in the telling of this history, we will also find Lesbian women who wore the black triangle of the asocials. 'Among the first women in Auschwitz were German prostitutes and Jewish girls from Slovaka. These women were issued evening gowns in which they were forced to help build Auschwitz in rain or snow. Of the hundreds, only a handful survived by 1944.'(15) Nun, queer, whore: think of the challenge posed to the unrestricted feminist historian and to all of us in our imaginations.

Both Lesbians and prostitutes were and are concerned with creating power and autonomy for themselves in seemingly powerless social interactions. As Bernard Cohen, one interviewer of working women has said, 'From the point of view of the prostitute, power and control must always be in her hands in order to survive.'(97) A Lesbian prostitute wrote in 1982, 'I'll make sure I'm out of there in 10 or 15 minutes. I'm always keeping my eye on the time and I decide how long I'll stay depending on the amount of money and what the guy is like . . . They want more, but in the end we set the terms of the relationship and the Johns have to accept it.' (Richards, LHA)

The class structure that exists for prostitutes also exists for Lesbians. The closer to the street you are, the more deviant you are seen. Call girls and professional Lesbian women have things in common. They both have more protection than the street walker or the bar dyke, but coming on to the wrong people can deliver each of them into the hands of the state. Both are often in a hurry to disconnect themselves from their sisters in the street in an effort to lighten their own feeling of difference.

At this point, Lesbians have more legal protection than prostitutes because of the power of the gay rights movement. We have Lesbian and gay elected public officials but no politicians who clearly claim their public sex past. Ruth Stout, a spokesperson for PONY – Prostitutes of New York – said in 1980 that if the hookers and the housewives and the homosexuals got together we could rule the world.(3) In order to do this, however, we must face the challenge of our own history, the challenge to understand how the 'Lesbian' world stretches from the flute players of Greece to the Michigan festival of Lesbian separatists. Why has this seemingly obvious connection between Lesbians and prostitutes remained so unspoken in our current Lesbian communities? What impact has cultural feminism and classism had on this silence? And will a reunion of these two histories give us a stronger political grasp on how to protect both prostitutes and Lesbians in this fearful time? If we can make any part of our society safer for these two groups of women, we will make the world safer for all women because whore and queer are the two accusations that symbolize lost womanhood and a lost woman is open to the direct control of the state.

The reclamation of one's history is a direct political act that forces the birth of a new consciousness; it is work that changes both the hearer and the speaker. I saw this very clearly when I attended the ground-breaking conference in Toronto last year. 'The Politics of Pornography. The Politics of Prostitution', and heard one of the keynote speakers, a stripper in Toronto's sex district, document the history of her art form in Toronto. Her telling created history as it communicated it. In her soft voice, she outlined the development of her profession and the oppression she and the others had to fight. It was a straightforward history filled both with pride and problems. I was sitting with two other strippers, and as Debbie documented the changes and challenges in their work, they sat on the edge of their seats. They told me later they had never heard it put that way. Out of dirty jokes and scorn, a history was born. I hope that more and more women who perform or work in the world of public sex will choose to tell their people's story.*

[Note: The collage method used in this paper has certain dangers that I want my readers to be aware of. The first is that I will dilute the historical specificity of each instance of connection because both the terms *Lesbian* and *prostitute* have their own socially constructed legacies. Second, because I have culled the references from a wide variety of sources and I am not an expert in any of the historical periods, I may oversimplify the resulting discoveries. However, I mean this work to be both factual and provocative, to break silences and to challenge assumptions, and most of all, to provide the materials for us all – the Lesbian, the prostitute, and the feminist (who may be all three) – to have a more caring complex understanding of each other so we can forge deeper and stronger bonds in the battles to come.]

I want to thank Margo St. James, Priscilla Alexander, and Gail Pheterson for their encouragement of my work and for their pioneer efforts in the prostitutes' rights movement.

Bibliography

Berube, Alan. From a manuscript sent to the Lesbian Herstory Archives (LHA).

Bullough, Vernon. 'Prostitution, Psychiatry and History', *The Frontiers of Sex Research*, Buffalo, NY, Prometheus Books, 1979.

Caprio, Frank. *Female Homosexuality: A Psychodynamic Study of Lesbianism*, New York, Grove Press, 1954.

---

*Patterned on the whore and feminist support groups of Holland, prostitutes, sex-trade workers, and feminists concerned with winning prostitutes' rights in this country are now in the process of organizing. Contact Coyote, Post Office Box 26354, San Francisco, California, 94126, for more information.

Cohen, Bernard. *Deviant Street Networks*, Lexington, KY, Lexington Books, 1980.

Falk, Candace. *Love, Anarchy and Emma Goldman*, New York, Holt, Rinehart and Winston, 1984.

Freedman, Estelle. *Their Sisters' Keepers: Women's Prison Reform in America 1830–1930*, Ann Arbor, Univ. of Michigan Press, 1981.

Hampton, Mabel. Tapes in possession of LHA.

Katz, Jonathan. *Gay/Lesbian Almanac: A New Documentary*, New York, Harper and Row, 1983.

Lasker, Vera, *Women in the Resistance and in the Holocaust: The Voice of Eyewitnesses*, Westport, Greenwood Press, 1983.

Maria. 'Maria: A Prostitute Who Loves Women', *Proud Woman*, 11 (March-April 1972) 4.

Millet, Kate. *The Prostitution Papers*, St Albans, NY, Paladin Books, 1975.

Otis, Leah Lydia. *Prostitution in Medieval Society*, Chicago, Univ. of Chicago Press, 1985.

Pearl, Cora. *Grand Horizontal*, New York, Stein and Day, 1983. First published in English, 1890.

Pheterson, Gail. *The Whore Stigma: Female Dishonor and Male Unworthiness*, Amsterdam, Ministerie van Socialé Zaken en Werkgelegenheid, 1986.

Richards, Terri. From a statement read by the author, a Lesbian prostitute, at 'Prostitutes: Our Life – Lesbian and Straight', a meeting in San Francisco, June 22, 1982. Organized by the U.S. Prostitution Collective.

Rosen, Ruth. *The Lost Sisterhood: Prostitution in America 1900–1918*, Baltimore, Johns Hopkins Univ. Press, 1982.

Sanger, William. *History of Prostitution: Its Extent, Causes and Effect Throughout the World*, New York, 1876.

Stern, Jess. *Sisters of the Night*, New York, Gramercy Publishers, 1956.

Streicher, Rikki. Excerpt from interview that appeared in *In The Life*, No. 1, Fall 1982. Publication of the West Coast Lesbian Collection, available at LHA.

Stout, Ruth. 'The Happier Hooker', *Daily News*, September 16, 1980.

Taylor, Katie. Interview, Spring, 1986.

Turrill, Barbara. 'Thirty Minutes in the Life', Transcript of talk for WGBH radio, May 13, 1976. Available at LHA.

Weeks, Jeffrey. *Coming Out*, London, The Anchor Press, 1977.

Woolston, H.B. *Prostitution in the United States Prior to the Entrance of the United States into the World War*, 1921. Reprinted, Montclair, New Jersey, Patterson-Smith, 1969.

When The Lions Write History

Things don't fall apart. Things hold.
Lines connect in thin ways that last and
last. Lines become generations made out
of pictures and words just kept.

Lucille Clifton, Generations

'**I** am glad the time has come when the "lions write history",' Wendell Phillips wrote to Frederick Douglass in 1845. 'We have been left long enough to gather the character of slavery from the evidence of the masters.' The Lesbian Herstory Archives is all about lions writing history. It is about a people's refusal to live within the dirty jokes and folklore pathology of a controlling society. To deprive a people of their history, or to construct one for them that immortalizes humiliation, is a conscious cultural act of the powerful.

In 1973, after being a Lesbian for fifteen years, I read a book that brought all the pieces of my life together: my life with my mother, a Jewish working-class woman who embezzled money and turned tricks to keep us together; my years on the barstools and bathroom line of the old Sea Colony bar; my years of teaching in the SEEK Program at Queens College where I learned about exile from generations of students. The book, *The Colonizer and the Colonized* by Albert Memmi, contained the following passage:

> The colonized draws less and less from her past. The colonizer never even recognized that she had one; everyone knows that the commoner whose origins are unknown has no history. Let us ask the colonized herself; who are her folk heroes? her great popular leaders? her sages? At most she may be able to give us a few names, in complete disorder

and fewer and fewer as one goes down the generations. The colonized seems condemned to lose her memory.

How could gay people have a memory of themselves as a people with a history when, for many years, our only social existence was on the pages of medical, psychological, legal and religious texts – all dedicated to proving our pathology. It is not that our people did not speak, but their words and their lives lived in the context of the colonizer. Now, after years of doing gay history work, we can go back to those early documents and liberate the men and women who are buried under the language of racism and homophobia.

From *Sex Variants*, published in 1948 by George Henry, a medical work containing case studies of eighty gay men and women:

Walter R.:
Father killed accidently when Walter was eleven. Walter adopted by wealthy English gentleman. Walter only colored boy in community. Timid. Protected by older boy who initiated him in homosexual relations. Foster father made advances. Walter shocked and disillusioned. Left home. Promiscuous homosexual relations. Maternal interest in boy. Alcoholism.

(Passive, effeminate homosexual.)

General impression: Walter is a large negro, tall and fairly heavy. His features are typical of his race. His forehead is receding, his nose flattened and prominent, his mouth large and his lips thick . . . He has many of the characteristics of a benign colored parson, a fussy spinster and a Southern mammy.

Marian J.:
Marian is a large, middle-aged mulatto woman of medium height. Her well-developed breasts and hips suggest the

gentle mammy but her square shoulders, erect posture, decisive gait and fearless attitude give the impression of being distinctly masculine attributes . . . For forty years Marian has been a professional entertainer and for twenty years she was a favorite in European society . . .

Hidden in these fragmented and racist descriptions are real people, the forefathers and mothers we search for. It is part of our responsibility as a people chronicling its own history to reclaim their colonized lives. Listen to the richness of Black Lesbian history contained in these excerpts from two *Jet* articles written in 1954:

'Women Who Pass for Men'
For thirty years, a hefty Mississippi woman lived as a man, sternly bossing a 10-acre farm and caring for an attractive cream-coloured 'wife' and her daughter by a previous marriage. When the man died two years ago, an amazed undertaker discovered that Pete Bell was really a woman.

At the wife's request, the masquerade was hushed and the burial certificate listed no sex . . . Incredulous citizens in the small town pooh-poohed the report, claiming 'old Pete just couldn't have fooled me'.

Very often the masquerade is only uncovered by an accident or a necessary visit to a doctor. After an automobile accident, Cincinnati doctors realized that 'Charles Harris' – who had posed as a man for forty-five years – was a woman. Harris' true sex was revealed to a woman who knew her as her step-father. Mrs Ida Belle Redd said Harris (who died recently in Cincinnati at the age of 107) married her mother in 1902.

'Women Who Fall For Lesbians'
Just why some women fall for Lesbians is perhaps best summed up in an observation made by writer-researcher Arthur Guy Matthews, who stated recently in a health

magazine: 'The lesbian makes a point of seeking out widows, lonesome women, the victims of broken love affairs, and those who have suffered from nervous breakdowns and other mental ills.'

One Missouri school teacher, for example, who found herself getting on in years without the comfort and companionship of a man, succumbed to the wily advances of a lesbian of similar age, and opened her home to her. They lived together in presumed 'spinsterhood' the remaining days of their lives. When the lesbian finally died of a heart attack, the then retired teacher, grief-stricken, soon followed her in death.

Similarly, a romance between a New York woman doctor and her nurse has been winked at and accepted by Harlem society for years.

It is tempting to focus our spotlight on the famous and accomplished, the men and women of letters, of theater, of politics. It is important to do this: think of the impact of public acknowledgment of Langston Hughes' gayness. But other voices also await us, small voices, announcing themselves in just a few lines in an early gay publication like the letter written to the *Mattachine Review* in 1959 by Mrs M.A. from New Jersey:

Review Editor:
It's taken me a great deal of courage to write this. What does one do in going about or how does one go about obtaining a homosexual partner? I am 38, stout, 190 lbs., coloring brown-skinned. I've written coloring because we colored usually do. Separated from my husband. How do you help normal people in their sex problems? Please keep this confidential. I work as a domestic here . . . New York is a very large city. There must be someone for me.

Or in a longer letter written to New York Daughters of Bilitis (DOB) in 1969:

Dear D.O.B. Sisters,

For some time now I have been receiving mail from you. I feel quite close to you through your newsletter. It is much like a letter from home each month. I would love to come to the meetings but my late working hours and our two small children at home make that quite impossible. My wife Delores and I feel we know all of you through your names and articles in the newsletter. Our neighborhood is not at all oriented to gay life, nor is there any gay socializing nearby . . .

In the beginning of 1969 we found ourselves pretty much in hot water. I had left a job in New York to live in Jersey with Delores. She wanted to move to New Jersey and so we did. Finding an apartment was pretty rough because I had not gotten settled in a job yet, but we did manage eventually to get into a housing project that was very nice for the kids and Delores . . . After all was settled, furniture and all, we set ourselves down to living normally again . . .

We sent Jean, our oldest, out to play and soon after she came home crying. A little girl she had been trying to play with told her her mother said not to play with her. After much comforting, we all settled down and shrugged it off. Time went on and soon we found out there had never been any lesbians in this project before, nor were there any 'known' lesbians in the area. Delores and I were almost totally ignored. Delores did have one or two who would say hello to her, but me they wouldn't speak to. I am very pronounced in my appearance, there is no mistaking me for what I am. I am a butch and Delores loves me that way . . . The men and women in the building seemed to feel that my appearance was a threat to them. Getting on the elevator with me was out of the question. With Delores, they would hesitate and get on anyway.

I believe to this day the only thing that helped was Delores' way with the house and children . . . Slowly she would run into a woman in the laundromat who might comment on how well-behaved the children were. Each time Delores would run home simply elated. Nothing could have been better than someone really talking to her. It was such a small thing but it meant so much. I thought I would ask her to move, but she said she is here and she will stay whether they liked it or not.

Then I decided I would take her out for a night, go to New York, be with other gay people for a while. She might feel better. Delores asked one of the teenage girls in the building if she would sit for the children that night. The girl said no first and then said that her mother had 'finally' consented. All was fine until the day after we went out. I came home and found Delores totally wrecked. It seems the girl went home after sitting for us and was asked by her mother if she was propositioned, molested, or asked to return when we both were home. Well, I think Delores' heart was broken . . .

Delores asked a woman one day if she wanted a ride to the store with her. The woman said alright as long as her husband did not know. Soon after we were known as pretty nice people but don't be alone with them. Each month passed until summer finally came and it is the habit of the women in this building to sit outside and talk. We passed this group of sun bathers quite often and usually the air was pretty tense or the conversations would cease. It was very heart-breaking for Delores. She had not wanted to be part of any gossip or coffee clotch [*klatsch*], but the complete withdrawal from her was I think a bit too much. My heart went out to her then as it does now when she does something really great, which is pretty often.

Slowly people started giving credit where it belonged. Delores and the kids won them over whether they liked it or not. One day the electricity went out. Our Jean walked a man all the way up to the twelfth floor holding his hand because he had a heart condition. Then the day came when Delores and I were giving a birthday party for Jean. The children were to come at 1:00 and leave at 3:00. The party lasted until eight o'clock. The kids just wouldn't go home.

The next day our phone rang constantly, mothers calling,

asking what we did. The children never stopped talking about how wonderful Delores and Lou Ellen were, how they loved us. From the mouths of babes came the answer.

Now when Delores and I go out the door, ten kids rush to kiss her hello and couldn't they please come with us? Today they know in this community that lesbians are not stag film replicas. Today when they need a good meat loaf recipe or their hair done, even an interior decorator or a baby sitter, they simply call on the two lesbians who moved up on the twelfth floor two years ago.

We all have our struggles. Isn't it just great when we make enough headway to walk into a restaurant and not have the waitresses huddle in a corner whispering, or walk down the theater aisle and everyone keeps watching the picture, or walk down a street unnoticed.

Love to all of you,
Delores, Lou Ellen, Jean, Peter

A quiet courage of desire and a rock-strong resistance lie at the heart of these documents, and in our history, a people's history, they serve as monuments to the thousands of other lives waiting for us to find them. Our history work must go on in the face of all the insanities around us. Racism and homophobia feed on the destruction of a people's selfhood: while they rant, we must continue piecing together the fullness of our story.

Angelina Grimke, a Black Lesbian writer of the Harlem Renaissance, calls to us, and her voice stands for a multitude:

The days fall upon me;
One by one, they fall,
Like Leaves . . .
They are black,
They are gray.
They are white.
They are shot through with gold and fire.
They fall,

They fall
Ceaselessly.
They cover me,
They crush,
They smother.
Who will ever find me
Under the days?

In this finding, we will also find ourselves and lay a hold on our own future. Memory is a people's gift to themselves, and for an oppressed, a hated people, it is the place where the collective soul takes refuge.

Besides the voices of individual lives, we also have documents of the social and political groups that fought the history forced on them. We learn in Jonathan Katz's *Gay American History* of the Los Angeles group, the Knights of the Clock, an interracial group of heterosexual and homosexual men and women who joined together in 1950 'with the aim of promoting understanding among homosexuals, between blacks and whites, and offering social, employment and housing services especially to interracial couples'. We can also remember in our collective gay minds the click of the police photographers' cameras as they photographed the six hundred gay people who had the courage to attend a dance given by an early homophile rights organization in San Francisco, six hundred faces frozen in time, but six hundred women and men that continued walking through that door into our history.

Our organizations come into being because brave women and men understand that we must take responsibility for the vitality and protection of all of our community. In September 1976, a group of Black Lesbian women wrote the following words:

The official name of this group is the Third World Gay Women's Organization. We call ourselves the Salsa-Soul Sisters.

We came into being because there was no other organization that we knew of in the New York area, existing for or dealing with the serious needs of third world gay women. We

175

started by searching out each other, because of the strong
needs we have in common, and to grow to understand the ways
in which we differ.

Our immediate aim is to provide a place where third world
gay sisters can meet other gay sisters, other than in bars.

We hope to become an organization of third world gay
women who feel joy as well as pride in being able to say, 'we
did it ourselves'. Meaning, we started, formed, maintained, and
governed an organization that is helpful and inspiring to third
world gay women. We share in the strengthening and produc-
tivity of the whole gay community.

Salsa-Soul fulfilled its promise, and these early words are
now a document of a people's vision and the courage to carry
it out.

Our history is made up of many histories – all the layers of identity that form our personhood, that connect us to legacies of
love and pride and pain. This is the deeper challenge to a
community that says yes, we come from different places but we
are queer and that is our bond. Respect for difference is more
than rhetoric; it is education about where one's soul lives. For
some of us there are historical symbols that make us wince
in collective pain, symbols that we cannot play with because
blood and servitude are wrapped in their folds. History will
betray us if we betray it. If we do not learn the language of each
other's historical truths, if we do not grow aware of the places
where life has been stolen, our histories and our lives will be
selfish things. This is one reason why your organization, Men
of All Colors Together, is so important.

Coalition politics is a desperately needed, deeply practical
strategy in these Reagan times. One of its goals is to extend
the boundaries of understood experiences so these boundaries
become less lonely, less the burden of one group and more the
recognized need of communities in partnership. You take this
strategy and turn it into lived lives. Politics becomes passion,
or perhaps passion becomes politics. One of the strongest gifts

you give this hate-filled society is proof that neither racism nor classism nor homophobia can silence a loving voice, nor stop a loving touch. I know this gift is not easily come by. I have read your newsletters and seen documented the hours of work and risk-taking. But you are changing history.

I write what some call erotica and others call pornography. I write it to celebrate the fineness and richness of sexuality, the complexity of women's desire, because it is at the center of our history as it is at the center of our oppression as gay people. That the state has decreed our love-making a crime, that each of us who touches his or her loved one, or enters him or her in that forbidden way, is open to legal punishment, depending on geography, should not surprise us after the initial shock of the Supreme Court decision has worn off. Is this not the same government that still refuses to stop the fascist nightmare of South Africa? Is this state that forbids our private love not the same one publicly declaring we will bring down the legal government of Nicaragua, that we will make possible the murder of men, women, and children because we disagree with their choices? Is this not the same state that brags about our prosperity while hundreds of thousands are homeless and foodless and hopeless? I know that all their decrees, all their appeals to their version of history, the ancient history of the hatred of sodomites, will not bring our Movement to a halt, but a toll will be taken. Our young people face the medical warnings and social stigma of AIDS on one side, and the legal warnings of the state on the other. Now, once again, our history and the history of all those who resisted must be made a living thing. It must give nourishment and dignity and strength. It must show all the nuances of resistance, and it must not leave anyone out.

From Stonewall to Soweto the people are resisting, and that chant and this struggle have brought us into new lands. History is not a dead thing or a sure thing. It lives with our choices and our dreams. It is the story of our glories and our sadnesses. It is at different times a lover, an enemy, a teacher, a prophet. It is always a collective memory as complicated and as contradictory as the people who lived it, but it is always a people's story. Let our tale be marked by our knowledge of what had to be done, and let it shine with the passion of our attempt.

Text of a speech given on July 5, 1986 at the Men of All Colors Convention in New York City.

Hope

Wearing my voluminous flannel nightgown, I knelt before the small wood-burning stove, trying to see why the fire was so fragile. I felt huge and awkward in that position, aware of my rump and falling breasts, but the cold night air demanded that the fire be encouraged to burn at a brisker pace. My younger lover, small and tight in her body, sat on the couch watching me. I did not like what I thought she saw. I did not like the bigness of my ass, the weight of my body on my knees, and then just as I worked very hard to accept my lack of appeal, she said in a low firm voice, 'You look so fuckable that way.'

I froze, caught in that moment of self-hatred by the clarity of her desire. I stopped all movement, awed once again by the possibilities of life. I knew she was walking toward me. I felt her stand behind me, felt her hands shape my nightgown to my curves. I heard her breath come quicker, and still I did not move. She grew impatient and reached under the gown, piling up its lengths on her arm like a fisherman pulling in his nets, and then against all my fear, she entered me. The fire blazed up, and so did my hope as I finally left the burden behind me and rode her hand with all the grace love had ever given me.